ISBN: 9781290656085

Published by:
HardPress Publishing
8345 NW 66TH ST #2561
MIAMI FL 33166-2626

Email: info@hardpress.net
Web: http://www.hardpress.net

THE FOOLS OF
SHAKESPEARE

Frederick Warde as "Cecco" in "The Duke's Jester"

THE FOOLS
OF SHAKESPEARE

An Interpretation of Their Wit,
Wisdom and Personalities

BY

FREDERICK WARDE

NEW YORK
McBRIDE, NAST & COMPANY
1913

Published, October, 1913

PREFACE.

Foolery, sir, does walk about the orb like the sun;
it shines everywhere.

How far the above epigram may apply to the
compiler of this work, may be a matter of opinion.

Among the legion of books dealing with the
characters of Shakespeare, I have found the majority
to be devoted to his tragic and serious creations,
a few to his humorous types, but none to
his fools.

In the course of a lengthy career upon the
stage, which has been chiefly devoted to the plays
of Shakespeare, I have witnessed the performance
of these fools by accomplished actors whose skill
has illuminated the text, and whose abilities have
vitalized the poet's creations till they lived in my
mind, not as imaginary beings, but as real men
who walked, talked, and gamboled before me.
I have listened to their words, laughed at their
wit, pondered on their wisdom, and have marveled

i

that their point and significance have apparently escaped the notice of so many readers and students.

This must be my excuse, if not my justification, for the book.

The matter was the subject of one of my lectures, under the title, "The Wit and Wisdom of Shakespeare's Fools" and included in my series "Shakespeare and His Plays." I found, however, the material so abundant I could not include it in the limited time at my command on the platform. I have therefore elaborated the theme, enlarged the scope of the design, and divided it into chapters, which I hope will entertain the reader, instruct the student, and prove of some interest generally.

I make no claim to originality, and have endeavored in all instances to credit the author with the thoughts I have quoted.

I have found occasion in several instances, to differ with some of the well known Shakespearean scholars; but it must always be remembered that I speak from the view-point of the actor, for whom, and for whom alone the plays were written.

I have not entered the literary dissecting room, nor invaded the realm of psychology. The line of demarcation between humor and imbecility, folly and insanity, I leave to the professional alienist.

I have taken the characters as they appear in the plays and as I conceive the author intended them, with due reference to their relation to the other characters.

I proceed upon the fact that Shakespeare, being an actor, wrote these plays to be acted. That his purpose was to create or draw the characters as he saw or imagined them for dramatic presentation. I believe their literary quality was a matter of comparative indifference to him, the creation of the plot, the conception of the characters, and the arrangements of the incidents being his first, if not his only consideration. The beauty of diction, the delicate imagery, the exquisite poetry, and the sublime philosophy, were the spontaneous expression of his transcendent but unconscious genius

Scan the records of the thoughts of men,
On graven stone, or papyrus leaf;
On parchment scroll or printed page,
Through all the eons of the ages past
To the high noontide of the passing day:
Then add the sum, and its grand total
Will be beggared by the genius of one name, alone.
Shakespeare!

FREDERICK WARDE.

CONTENTS

ILLUSTRATIONS

THE FOOLS OF SHAKESPEARE

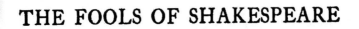

INTRODUCTION

The somewhat trite old adage, "It takes a wise man to make a fool," is familiar to us all, but the full point and significance of the proverb is only comprehended by those who are familiar with mediæval history, romance, or poetry.

Its apparent inconsistency, however, is founded upon a substantial basis of reason, and a brief relation of mediæval conditions will show the truth of the adage, and the point of its application.

In the early and middle ages it was customary for a monarch, prince, or a powerful noble to have in his retinue or household a fool or jester, whose office was to entertain and amuse his master and his friends. He was quite an important personage; enjoyed privileges, and was permitted liberties that were denied the greatest nobles, the closest friends, or the nearest kindred of his master.

Nor birth nor rank were immune from the jests

and pranks of "The Jester," the monarch himself often bearing with good humor the jibes that would have cost the life of one less privileged. The fool was, however, exempt, upon the principle that "There is no slander in an allowed fool." Usually a favorite with his master, his influence was sought in many a state and court intrigue, for under the cloak of folly he could by tale or parable, tell his patron truths that others could not or would not speak, and approve or ridicule any scheme or project that his interest or wishes might desire. However plain his truths or bitter his satire few were rash enough to retaliate, and woe to that noble or courtier who might incur the enmity or displeasure of the fool, for he would become the target of his wit and the butt of his jests, with little hope of redress, or opportunity for revenge.

The life of a jester was a lonely one: he was subject to the caprices of his master, contemned above the board, hated below it, yet feared by all.

To play such a part successfully required a man

of more than ordinary wisdom. He could not be without learning. He must be a man of great observation, judgment, and understanding; quick to take advantage of every occasion for the exercise of his wit, with judgment of the time, and discretion as to what to say as well as what to leave unsaid.

Times have changed. Progress and evolution have brought new conditions; folly no longer carries a bauble, and the man who was wise enough to wear the motley of the mediæval fool might don to-day the robe of the justice or the toga of the statesman with dignity to the office and honor to himself.

The requirements of a court fool are well described by Viola in "Twelfth Night," Act 3, Sc. 1.

> This fellow's wise enough to play the fool,
> And to do that well craves a kind of wit:
> He must observe their mood on whom he jests,
> The quality of persons, and the time,
> And, like the haggard, check at every feather
> That comes before his eye. This is a practice
> As full of labor as a wise man's art;
> For folly that he wisely shows is fit,
> But wise men, folly-fallen, quite taint their wit.

The dress of the fool was a motley or parti-colored doublet and hose, with the arms of the house to which he belonged embroidered on the breast or thigh; his head-dress, a hood parti-colored like his coat, and surmounted by a cocks-comb; his emblem, which he always carried, was a lath or short staff, headed by a miniature hood and cockscomb similar to his own called a bauble, and was as sacred to the fool as the sword to the soldier, or the crest to the knight. The bauble also served as a protection, and rendered him immune from the anger of those whom he might offend—for, to strike the fool was considered the act of a coward. The cap, bauble, and points of the jester's dress were adorned with small bells that jingled as he moved, and gave warning of his approach.

Jaques, in "As You Like It," thus enumerates the privileges of a fool:

O, that I were a fool!
I am ambitious for a motley coat.

. . . .

I must have liberty
Withal, as large a charter as the wind,

To blow on whom I please: for so fools have:
And they that are most galled with my folly,
They must most laugh. And why, sir, must they so?
The "why" is plain as way to parish church:
He, that a fool doth very wisely hit,
Doth very foolishly, although he smart,
Not to seem senseless of the bob; if not
The wise man's folly is anatomis'd
Even by the squandering glances of the fool.
Invest me in my motley: give me leave
To speak my mind, and I will through and through
Cleanse the foul body of the infected world,
If they will patiently receive my medicine.

The jester was not usually a gentleman, but history records several instances where men of gentle birth and breeding have filled the office: sometimes from design or policy, and sometimes because of physical infirmities which rendered them incapable of bearing arms, or prevented them from taking part in feats of chivalry in field or tourney. Not infrequently the jester was a dwarf or cripple, his deformity giving a grotesqueress to his appearance and grim point to his satire.

Dr. Doran, in his "History of Court Fools," gives us the following legend, as the origin of the character, and the office:

Once upon a time, it happened that all Olympus was dull and the gods were moping about, simply bored to death. It was a warm summer day and in a distant valley below they could see a group of Greek peasants disporting on the green turf in gala attire. The happy rustics were dancing and singing, enjoying the bright sunshine, and the sounds of their mirth floated up faintly to the gods in a manner that was altogether offensive to them.

"Omnipotent Father," cried Mercury, ill-naturedly, "it would be rare sport, O king of gods and men, to scatter all these gaily-robed revelers, and by a shower spoil their finery and their fun."

The suggestion was enthusiastically received by the assembled deities.

"I propose an amendment," exclaimed Juno, with feminine sympathy. "Before you send the rain, let your priest from the shrine below announce to the people that a shower is about to descend, but it shall wet only fools."

Zeus, approving, a slight sound of thunder was heard, and the priest stood in front of the altar and made the requisite announcement to the people. Only one of the Greeks took the precaution to go into his house. Every other man waited to see the fools drenched, and every man there was in two minutes wet to the skin. When the sun reappeared the man who had sought shelter came out of doors and laughed at his drenched and disconcerted fellows, who, angered at his dry and comfortable condition, fell upon him and beat him severely, calling him "a fool" and the like. Bruised and battered, he defended himself as well as he could, crying, "Have patience but a moment, and I will prove to you that I am not such a fool as I look." His tormentors paused, and he, looking upward, fell on his knees, exclaiming:

"O, Zeus, merciful and just, send down another shower; wet me to the skin even as these fools are wet, make me as great a fool as my neighbors and enable me, a fool, to live at peace among fools."

Down came the shower prayed for, and the two assemblies, the gods above and the fools below, roared with laughter, as he stood there drenched to the skin like the rest. "This is unjust," cried

Juno, as the laughter ceased, "and you have spoiled that good fellow's robe."

"True," replied Zeus, "but with that shower I bestowed upon him wit, wisdom, and humor, and have breathed that fact into the ear of the chief of the district, who will take this humorous philosopher home with him, to be at once his diverter and instructor."

That night at a banquet given by the chief, the wise fool stood near his master, pouring out witty truths as fast as his lips could utter them, and the gods both envied the fun and admired the wisdom. "That fellow," cried Zeus, "shall be the founder of a race. Henceforward each court shall have its fool; and fools shall be the preachers and admonishers of kings. Children," he added, to the gods and goddesses, raising a goblet of nectar, "here's a health to the first of fools."

THE FOOLS OF SHAKE-
SPEARE

THE FOOL IN LIFE AND IN
LITERATURE

HISTORY records the names of a number of men who in the character of court fool have made themselves famous both in word and deed. Of these one of the most distinguished was Triboulet, court jester to King Francis I, of France. Triboulet was a nickname, but we know no other. He was deformed in body, ludicrous in appearance, but of a very brilliant mind. His wisdom was equal to his wit, and he was, at times, both fool and adviser to the king. Francis was deeply attached to him and he returned the affection loyally. Much of his wit is recorded, and his pranks at the meeting of his master with King Henry VIII, of England, at the "Field of the cloth of gold," are related in the chronicles of that brilliant spectacle.   It is of Triboulet that the following bon mot is related.   He had offended a powerful nobleman of the court, who, in retaliation, threatened to hang him.   As the nobleman was a man of his word, poor Triboulet's life was in danger, so he went to the king and told him of the threat.

"Never fear, Triboulet," said the king, "if he hangs you, I'll hang him fifteen minutes afterwards."

To this Triboulet replied, "Couldn't your Majesty contrive to hang him fifteen minutes before?"

Two other French fools of distinction were Brusquet and Chicot. The former held the office of jester to three kings, Henri II, Francis II, and Charles IX; while the latter was the friend and fool to Henri III.

The most prominent English court fools or jesters were: Will Sommers, in the reign of Henry VIII; Patch, attached to the household of Cardinal Wolsey; Heywood, at the court of Queen Mary; and Dick Tarleton, at that of Eliz-

abeth. Heywood, however, was also a dramatist of some distinction, and Tarleton, a very pop-
ular-comic actor of the period. Later we find
Archie Armstrong, at the court of James I; and
Tom Killigrew, who besides being jester was
"Master of the Revels," to Charles I. The latter is described by Pepys as "a merry droll, but
a gentleman of great esteem with the king."
Killigrew was probably the last of the licensed
court fools, and the office of household jester
ceased to exist, the character subsequently degen-
erating into the itinerant merry-andrew, a buffoon
who appeared at country fairs and village festi-
vals, and is now seen only at Christmas time with
the mummers that accompany the waits and carol
singers in old-fashioned English villages.

In romance the fool has prominently figured,
always with picturesque and frequently with dramatic effect.

Sir Walter Scott, in his romantic novel "Ivan-
hoe," has described with much detail and fidelity
the character of "Wamba," and has given us a
very accurate and impressive picture of the life

and characteristics of the jester-minstrel of the time of Richard Cœur-de-Lion.

We are indebted to Victor Hugo, in "Le Roi s'ammuse," for a striking and powerful picture of the Italian court fool. The character is more familiar, perhaps, in a dramatic version of the same story, called "The Fool's Revenge," by Tom Taylor, in which the late Edwin Booth gave such a wonderfully effective presentation of the poor deformed jester Bertuccio, concealing under the motley garb and mocking tones of the fool the intensity of a father's love.

The French court fool is most picturesquely presented in "La Dame de Monsereau," in which the elder Dumas has woven a very interesting and exciting romance around the character of "Chicot," jester to King Henry III. Chicot is represented as a gallant soul, full of honor and chivalry, as ready with his sword as with his wit, both being equally effective. The romance was dramatized for me recently, under the title of "The Duke's Jester," by Mr. Espey Williams, who transferred the scene of action from the court

Edwin Booth as "Bertuccio" in "The Fool's Revenge"

of France to that of the Duke of Milan, in Italy;
and changed the name of "Chicot" to "Cecco."
I played the part of the jester with some success,
and retained the play in my repertoire for several
years.

In the drama we have an admirably constructed
and splendidly written play, "Francesca di Rimini," by the late George Boker, where we find
the fool "Pepe," keen of wit, but depraved in
mind, a very "Iago" in motley. His fun is malicious, his humor mischievous and his wit malev-
olent. A masterly performance of the character
was given by my friend and comrade, Mr. Louis
James, with whose name it will always be
identified.

It is Shakespeare, however, who has given us
the best types of fool, in which may be found not
only wit and wisdom, but all of those qualities
I have endeavored to enumerate. He has left us
enduring pictures of mediæval life and manners,
that make the characters live again in their true
and perfect body and environment.

Of pertinent interest after this brief sketch of

the historical position of the fool is the interpretation of Shakespeare's fools contained in a posthumous work by Francis Douce, published in London in 1839, entitled "Illustrations from Shakespeare." There I find a chapter of about twenty pages with the caption: "Desertation I., The character of Shakespeare's fools."

My knowledge of this work was obtained from Mr. Wilfred Clarke, a son of the late eminent comedian, John Sleeper Clarke, who found the manuscript of the extracts, printed below, in the property room of the old Walnut Street Theater in Philadelphia, while he was examining some papers and effects of his deceased father. The MSS. was written, I have subsequently learned, by Mary Ann Booth, and is in a fine hand, on old-fashioned blue note paper, now soiled and discolored with age, and dogs-eared as if from frequent use and reference.

In the printing of the excerpts I have retained the capitalizing of the words and the punctuation as I found it in the MSS. as characteristic of the writer and the period.

I cannot agree with several of the propositions advanced by the author, and it may be interesting to know that on its first publication the book met with severe condemnation at the hands of the critics, so much so, that the author withdrew it from sale, and it was not republished till some five years after the author's death.

The significance of this little manuscript lies in the evidence it gives us of the study and research that such an actor as the late Mr. Clarke gave to the accurate presentation of his characters, fools and clowns though they were. The details of the various kinds of fools may also be noted with interest, as well as the difference of the kind and quality of the costumes worn by these attractive men of motley.

I. THE GENERAL DOMESTIC FOOL.

(Often but as it should seem improperly termed "a clown.")

He was—1. A mere natural or idiot.
        2. Silly by nature, yet cunning and sarcastical.
        3. Artificial

Puttenham speaking of the latter, says— A buffoune or counterfeit foole, to hear him speake wisely which is like himself, it is no sport at all; but for such a counterfeit to talk and looke foolishly it maketh us laugh, because it is no part of his natural.

All i' officiated occasionally as menial servants.

t Fool belonged to this 3rd class.

e ate and disordinate joy became incorpo-
body of a jeaster; this fellow in person is
, in appearell courtly, but in behaviour a very
and no man; his studie is to coine bitter jests, or to shew antique motions, or to sing baudie ballads: give him a little wine in his head, he is continually flearing and making of mouthes: he laughs intemperately at every little occasion, and dances about the house, leaps over tables, outskips mens heads, trips up his companions heels, burns sack with a candle, and hath all the feats of a lord of misrule in the country: feed him in his humour, you shall have his heart, in meere kindness he will hug you in his armes, kisse you on the cheek, and rapping out an horrible oath, crie God's soul Tom, I love you, you know my poore heart, come to my chamber for a pipe of tobacco, there lives not a man in this world that I more honour. In these ceremonies you shall know his courting, and it is a speciall mark of him at the table, he sits and makes faces: keep not this fellow company, for in jugling with him, your wardropes shall be wasted, your credits crackt, your crownes consumed, and time

(the most precious riches of the world) utterly lost. This is the picture of a real hireling or artificial fool, from a singular tract entitled "Wit's miserie," 1599.

It is so exceedingly clear that the terms clown and fool were used, however improperly, as synonymous of our old writers that it would be an unnecessary occupation of the reader's time to adduce examples. Their confused introduction in the dramatis personæ might indeed render this position doubtful to any one who had not well considered the matter; but although the fool of our old plays denoted either a witty hireling or artificial fool, both retained for the purpose of making sport for their employers, the clown was certainly a character of much greater variety. He occasionally represented one of the above personages; sometimes he was a mere rustic, and very often no more than a shrewd and witty domestic. There are some instances in which any low-character in a play served to amuse the audiences with his sallies of coarse buffoonery, and thus became the clown of the piece. In short, the theatrical clown or fool seems to have been a kind of heterogeneous character, drawn in part from real life, but very considerably heightened to produce stage effect; an opinion that derives considerable support from what Shakespeare has put into the mouth of Hamlet, when he makes him admonish those who play the clowns to speak no more than is set down for them. Indeed, the great dramatist himself cannot be absolved from the imputation of having given too high a colouring to the characters in question, unless we suppose, what is ex-

tremely probable, that his plays have been very much
interpolated by the extemporaneous nonsense of the
players.

Dr. Fuller, speaking of the Court Jester, whom he
says some count a necessary evil, remarks in his usual
quaint manner, that it is an office which none but he
that hath wit can perform, and none but he that wants
it will perform.

THE CLOWN.

1. A mere country booby.
2. A witty rustic.
3. Any servant of a shrewd and witty disposition,
and who, like a similar character in our modern plays,
was made to treat his master with great familiarity
in order to produce stage effect.

III. The female fool, who was generally idiot.

IV. The City or Corporation Fool, whose office was
to assist at public entertainments and in pageants. To
this class belong perhaps the Lord Mayor's state fool,
and those employed by the companies of trades &c.

V. Tavern Fools. These seem to have been retained to amuse the customers. We learn from one
of Ben Jonson's plays that they exhibited with the
jews harp, mounted on a joint-stool, and in another of
them he has preserved the name of such a character:
they were sometimes qualified to sing after the Italian
manner. Fools were also employed in the common
brothels.

VI. The Fool of the ancient theatrical mysteries and
moralities. He was more properly speaking, the Vice

a singular character, that would afford matter for much better dessertations than those of Warburton and Upton. Being generally dressed in a fool's habit, he appears to have been gradually and undistinguishably blended with the domestic fool; yet he was certainly a buffoon of a different sort. He was always a bitter enemy to the Devil, and a part of his employment consisted in teazing and tormenting the poor fiend on every occasion. He ceased to be in fashion at the end of the sixteenth century.

VII. The Fool in the old dumb shows exhibited at fairs, and perhaps at inns, in which he was generally engaged in a struggle with death; a fact that seems alluded to more than once in Shakespeare's plays. It is possible that some casual vestiges of this species of entertainment might have suggested the modern English pantomimes.

VIII. The Fool in the Whitsun ales and Morris dance.

IX. The Mountebank's fool, or Merry Andrew.

There may be others introduced into our old dramas of an indefinite and irregular kind, and not reducible to any of the above classes.

COSTUME.

Whoever is desirous of obtaining general and accurate information concerning the great variety of dresses that belong to some of the characters in question at different periods, must study ancient prints and paintings, and especially the miniatures that embellished manuscripts. These will furnish sufficient specimens; but the difficulty of ascertaining how the theatrical fools and clowns of Shakespeare's time were always habited, is insuperable. In some instances the plays themselves assist by peculiar references that leave but little doubt; but this is not the case in general.

It may be collected both from the plays themselves, and from various other authorities, that the costume of the domestic fool in Shakespeare's time was of two sorts.

(Here follow some etchings in pencil.)

On the first of these the coat was motley or parti-coloured, and attached to the body by a girdle, with bells at the skirt and elbows, though not always. The breeches and hose close, and sometimes each leg of a different colour. A hood resembling a monk's cowl, which at a very early period, it was certainly designed to imitate, covered the head entirely, and fell down over part of the breast and shoulders. It was sometimes decorated with asses' ears, or else terminated in the neck and head of a cock, a fashion as old as the fourteenth century. It had often the comb or crest only of the animal.

The fool usually carried in his hand an official sceptre or bauble, which was a short stick ornamented at the end with the figure of a fool's head, or sometimes with that of a doll or puppet. To this instrument there was frequently annexed an inflated skin or bladder, the form of it varied. It was not always filled with air, but occasionally with sand or peas.

⟋ The other dress, and which appears to have been more common in the time of Shakespeare, was the long petticoat. This originally appertained to the idiot or natural fool. Why it came to be used for the allowed fool is not apparent. It was like the first, of various colours, the materials often costly, as of velvet, and guarded or fringed with yellow. In one instance we have a yellow leather doublet.

TRINCULO.

The character of Trinculo, who in the dramatis personæ is called a jester, is not very well discriminated in the course of the play itself. As he is only associated with Caliban and the drunken butler, there was no opportunity of exhibiting him in the legitimate character of a professed fool: but at the conclusion of the play it appears he was in the service of the King of Naples as well as Stephano. He must be regarded as an allowed domestic buffoon, and habited in the usual manner.

LAUNCE AND SPEED.

The character of Speed is that of a shrewd witty servant. Launce is something different, exhibiting a mixture of archness and rustic simplicity. There is no allusion to dress, nor any other circumstance that marks them as the domestic fool or jester.

THE CLOWN—FESTE.

This clown is a domestic or hired fool, in the service of Olivia. He is specially termed "an allowed fool" and "Feste, the jester, that the Lady Olivia's father took much delight in." Malvolio likewise speaks of him as "a set fool." Of his dress it is impossible to speak correctly. If the fool's expression "I will impeticoat thy greatility," be the original language, he must have been habited accordingly. Mr. Ritson has asserted that he has neither coxcomb nor bauble, deducing his argument from the want of any allusion to them. Yet such an omission may be a very fallacious guide in judging of the habit of this character on the stage. It must, however, be admitted that where this happens there can be no clue as to the precise manner in which the fool was dressed.

MEASURE FOR MEASURE—THE CLOWN.

The clown in this play officiates as the tapster of a brothel; whence it has been concluded that he is not a domestic fool, nor ought to appear in the dress of that character. A little consideration will serve to shew that the opinion is erroneous, that this clown is altogether a domestic fool, and that he should be habited accordingly. Many ancient prints furnish instances of the common use of the domestic fool in brothels.

LOVE'S LABOUR'S LOST—THE CLOWN.

The clown in this play is a mere country fellow. The term "fool" applied to him in Act V, Sc. II, means nothing more than a silly fellow. He has not sufficient simplicity for a natural fool, nor wit enough for an artificial one.

LAUNCELOT GOBBO.

There is not a single circumstance through the whole of this play which constitutes Launcelot an allowed fool or jester; and yet there is some reason for supposing that Shakespeare intended him as such, from his being called a patch, a fool of Hagar's offspring, and in one place the fool. It is not reasonable, however, to conclude that a person like Shylock would entertain a domestic of this description; and it is possible that the foregoing terms may be merely designed as synonymous with the appellation of clown, as in "Love's Labour's Lost." On the whole we have here a proof that Shakespeare has not observed that nice discrimination of character in his clowns for which some have given him credit.

TOUCHSTONE.

Touchstone is the domestic fool of Frederick the duke's brother, and belongs to the class of witty or allowed fools. He is threatened with the whip, a mode of chastisement which was often inflicted on this motley personage. His dress should be a particoloured garment. He should carry a bauble in his hand, and wear asses ears to his hood, which is probably the head-dress intended by Shakespeare, there being no allusion whatever to the cock's head or comb.

ALL'S WELL THAT ENDS WELL.

The clown is a domestic fool of the same kind as Touchstone.

THE WINTER'S TALE.

The clown is a mere country booby.

KING LEAR.

The fool of this play is the genuine domestic buffoon; but notwithstanding his sarcastical flashes of wit, for which we must give the poet credit, and ascribe them in some degree to what is called stage effect, he is a mere natural with a considerable share of cunning. Thus Edgar calls him an innocent, and every one will immediately distinguish him from such a character as Touchstone. His dress on the stage should be particoloured; his hood crested either with a cock's comb to which he often alludes, or with the cock's head and neck. His bauble should have a head like his own with a grinning countenance for the purpose of exciting mirth in those to whom he occasionally presents it.

YORICK

"The King's Jester"

HAMLET, a young Danish prince, accompanied by his friend Horatio, stands by a low wall that encloses a graveyard watching an old sexton who is digging a grave. With professional unconcern the old fellow shovels out the earth, together with some human bones; amongst them two skulls, one of which he strikes smartly with his spade to imbed it in the soft earth, and prevent its rolling away.

Shocked at the apparent indifference of the old man to these dead relics, the prince advances, interrupts his work, and engages him in conversation. The grave-digger is a quaint, independent old fellow, and answers the prince's questions with humorous bluntness. The prince inquires, "How long will a man lie in the earth ere he rot?" After replying to the question, the sexton picks up one of the skulls from the mound of earth and asserts, "This skull hath lain i' the earth three-and-twenty years." "Whose was it?" asks the prince. "A whoreson mad fellow's it was," replies the sexton, and then adds, "A pestilence on him for a mad rogue! a' poured a flagon of Rhenish on my head once. This same skull, sir, was Yorick's skull, the king's jester."

Gently taking the grim remainder from the irreverent hands of the old grave-digger, and gazing at it with loving tenderness, the prince exclaims: "Alas, poor Yorick!—I knew him, Horatio: a fellow of infinite jest, of most excellent fancy: he hath borne me on his back a thousand times; and now how abhorred in my imagination it is! my gorge rises at it. Here hung those lips that I have kissed, I know not how oft. Where be your gibes now? your gambols? your songs? your flashes of merriment, that were wont to set the table in a roar? Not one now to mock your own grinning! quite chap-fallen!"

For three-and-twenty years that skull had la in the earth, till every vestige of its personali had been destroyed, and only the experienced eye of the old sexton could recognize it.

A chapless skull! dust and bones tossed up from the decaying earth from which they sprang, and to which, by the inexorable law of nature, they had returned; a skull that once was covered with skin and tissues, through which ran a myriad of arteries and veins, conveying the blood to and from the active brain that lay in the now empty shell. A skull that had crowned a frame, clothed like itself, intersected with nerves that connected the sensations of heart and brain, and canals that carried the vital fluids on their ceaseless course, giving the entire structure a living entity, and an individual personality; the personality of Yorick, jester to the court of Hamlet, King of Denmark.

Yorick! what a merry, loving soul he must have been, how full of fun and frolic. What pranks he must have played on those big, good-natured, long-haired Viking warriors, as they sat at the banquet table in the great hall of the castle of Elsinore. In fancy, I can hear their laughter at his madcap jests, and the deep roar of their

voices as they join in the chorus of his merry
songs.

I can see him in the churchyard, serious for a
moment, sitting on an ancient tombstone, gravely
watching the old sexton digging "a pit of clay";
the last resting place of folly and wisdom;
but his fun-loving soul cannot long be restrained
by even such solemn environment; so, furtively,
the mad rogue purloins the bibulous old grave
digger's flagon of Rhenish, standing near-by, and
pours its contents over the head of the discomfited
sexton; then, fleet as a deer he runs away, leaps
the churchyard wall, and the faint echo of his
merry laughter is the only solace for the old man's
wrath.

Yorick! the lines are few, and the description
brief that Shakespeare has given us of the man,
but they are so pregnant with suggestion, so sweet
in thought, and so tender in memory that he lives
in our minds as completely as though he gamboled
on the earth again, and laughingly jingled his cap
and bells in our very ears.

How happy must have been those early days

at Elsinore, when Hamlet was a child and Yorick
his play-fellow. How they must have romped
together in the gardens. What fun it was for the
little prince to climb upon the jester's shoulders
and race pick-back along the terraces, the boy's
long fair curls blowing in the wind, and his merry
laughter filling the air with music.. How pleasant to sit in the shade of one of the big old trees
in the park, and listen to the jester tell such interesting tales of the folklore of the country; of the
traditions of the prince's warlike race, and the
mighty deeds of his great Viking ancestors. Then
there were stories, too, wonderful stories, of goblins, sprites and fairies who did such strange
things that the relation of them almost frightens
the little prince; but he is reassured by a smile,
and, twining his arms round dear old Yorick's
neck, and kissing the jester's lips, he nestles close
to the breast of his motley friend in confident
security.

Three-and-twenty years have passed since then;
years of sorrow, years of pain! The prince is now
a man, with more than a man's share of doubts,

perplexities and cares: and yet at the sight of the bare, chapless skull of his dead play-fellow all the sweet and tender past comes back again.

What a tender pathos is mingled with the prince's philosophic reflections on the remains of his dead friend, as memory recalls each word and incident.   It is indeed a reflex of Yorick himself, as the prince utters the grim jest, "Now get you to my lady's chamber, and tell her, let her paint an inch thick, to this favor she must come."

So must we all! The king lies in his marble sepulcher, the jester in his humble grave in the churchyard: but the ermine robe and motley coat, the crown and bauble will mingle their dust, and find equality in the universal democracy of death.

TOUCHSTONE

"A Worthy Fool"

TO term Touchstone a clown, as he is called in the cast of characters of "As You Like It," seems to me both a misnomer and an injustice. His knowledge, his wisdom, his wit and his faculty of observation, raise him far above the condition that such a term would imply.

Fool to the court of The Duke, whose dukedom is not named, the character of Touchstone is a most positive and complete conception of the mediæval jester, and he more fully realizes the accomplishments essential to that office, as described by Viola in the "Twelfth Night," than any other of the motley-minded gentlemen that the poet has created.

He is a man of considerable learning, his wit is never lacking in wisdom, he chooses the object of his jests with prudence, the time with discretion, the matter with judgment, and he is never at a loss for a reply that is apt and to the point.

Touchstone scorns mere persiflage, is happily free from the punning habit, and is seldom a corrupter of words; he makes his jests by logical deductions, with a good premise, a sound argument, and a positive conclusion.

This same happy quality may be found in his encounters with the gentlemen of the court, the ladies in their disguises, the simple shepherds in the forest, and with the grave philosopher Jaques; indeed, it is the latter gentleman who most accurately summarizes the accomplishments, and gives the keynote to the jester's character, when he presents him to the Duke: "Is not this a rare fellow, good my lord? he is as good at anything, and yet a fool."

The wit of Touchstone does not scintillate, but burns with a steady flame; it is not like the sparks that fly from the contact of tempered steel, but the bright and ruddy glow that radiates from molten metal in the crucible. It is sententious rather than brilliant, more philosophic than frivolous, and invariably epigrammatic. His humor is never malicious, nor his satire bitter; he shoots his wit at every mark that presents itself, but his shafts are harmless; they have no barb and leave no sting.

Touchstone is not a buffoon, he does not play practical jests nor indulge in such pranks as did that "mad rogue" Yorick. Had it been Touchstone in the churchyard at Elsinore when the sexton was digging a grave, he would not have poured a flagon of wine over the old grave-digger's head; he would probably have leaned against one of the old yew trees, watched the proceedings with quiet reflection, and if the old sexton had advanced any of his socialistic theories, the jester would have argued the matter to the end, and no doubt have beaten him on his own proposition.

There are no demonstrations or expressions of affection by Touchstone, as by the fool in "King Lear," yet he is not lacking in loyalty; he leaves the court of Duke Frederick to follow the fortunes of Celia, the Duke's daughter, out of sincere regard, running the risk of the Duke's displeasure and probably of punishment if discovered; he accepts the fatigues of the journey and the discomforts of life in the forest of Arden without hesitation or complaint; he readily adapts himself to his new environment, keeps his own counsel, as well as that of his mistress, and holds the secret of the disguises of Celia and Rosalind inviolate.

My first acquaintance with Touchstone was made many years ago, at Manchester, in England. A very elaborate production of "As You Like It" was presented at the Prince's Theater there. I played the part of Orlando to the Rosalind of that beautiful and incomparable actress, Miss Adelaide Neilson. Mr. Compton was the fool. I cannot imagine a more adequate and effective performance of the part than Mr. Compton gave; his quaint personality, his unctuous humor, his artistic instinct, added to his ripe experience, combined to present a complete embodiment of the poet's design. The mobility of his features reflected the spirit of every line he uttered; and though he seldom smiled, under the gravity of his expression you seemed to feel there was the keenest appreci-

James Lewis as "Touchstone" in "As You Like It"

ation of the humor of the occasion, which laughter would have failed to convey.

The memory of Mr. Compton's performance will ever remain with me as the living embodiment of Touchstone.

It is a pleasing pastime to conjure up in one's mind the pictures that Shakespeare has drawn, and give them vitality, form and color. I have endeavored to imagine the scene of the first meeting of Touchstone with the gloomy philosopher Jaques, in the forest, as described by that eccentric gentleman.

> A fool, a fool! I met a fool i' the forest,
> A motley fool!—a miserable world!
> As I do live by food, I met a fool
> Who laid him down and bask'd him in the sun
> And rail'd on Lady Fortune in good terms,
> In good set terms, and yet a motley fool.

The description is brief, but it suggests to the imagination a scene of rare sylvan beauty, and striking human contrast. An opening in the trees where the sun, unimpeded by the heavy foliage of the deep forest brightens the landscape, and the atmosphere is redolent with the fragrance of the

wildwood flowers.   The bees are humming drows-
ily, the birds flit by on speedy wings to reach their
nests, and from their leafy homes trill out their
joy in sweetest melody.   Touchstone is lying
upon the soft green turf; he imagines himself to
be alone, unseen, unheard.   He is soliloquizing,
speaking his thoughts aloud, as many thinkers do,
possibly contrasting the beauties of nature with
which he is environed, with the frowns of fortune
that have banished his mistress and himself from
the luxurious life of the court to the plain, homely
existence in the primitive forest.   But he is not
alone.   Jaques, wandering through the forest, observes the motley figure reclining on the ground,
and hearing his voice but seeing no auditor, stops
and listens.   Noting his motley coat, Jaques at
first takes the fellow for an ordinary fool, for
which most people at that time, including Shakespeare himself, had a profound contempt; but
Touchstone's railing is no ordinary abuse; it is in
such "good terms," such "good set terms,"
that the philosopher not only stops to listen to
"the motley fool," but is so entertained that he

finally accosts, and greets him with a salutation that invites conference.

After the greeting there is another picture. The background is the same, but the figures have changed their position. The fool is still lying upon the ground, now alert and responsive; while Jaques has found the trunk of a friendly tree, against which he leans in contemplative curiosity.

It would be interesting to hear the whole of the dialogue between the recumbent fool and the standing philosopher; but the dramatist was too wise to make such an error of construction. He gives us the main points and leaves the rest to the imagination. That Touchstone was fully equal to the occasion, and "vented from the strange places in his brain, crammed with observation, mangled forms" that impressed and astonished "Good Monsieur Melancholy," is proved by the fact that the latter's usual gravity is changed to the broadest merriment, culminating in his expressed desire to emulate the province of the clown.

O that I were a fool!
I am ambitious for a motley coat.

But to return to that portion of this interesting
interview the poet has given us. It is narrated
by Jaques himself:

"Good morrow, fool," quoth I. "No, sir," quoth he,
"Call me not fool till heaven hath sent me fortune."
And then he drew a dial from his poke,
And looking on it with lack-lustre eye,
Says very wisely, "It is ten o'clock;
Thus may we see," quoth he, "how the world wags.
'Tis but an hour ago since it was nine,
And after one hour more 'twill be eleven;
And so, from hour to hour, we ripe and ripe,
And then from hour to hour we rot and rot;
And thereby hangs a tale." When I did hear
The motley fool thus moral on the time,
My lungs began to crow like chanticleer,
That fools should be so deep-contemplative,
And I did laugh sans intermission
An hour by his dial.—O noble fool!
A worthy fool! Motley's the only wear.

We are not informed of the effect of the interview on Touchstone but, doubtless, like a good
soldier that appreciates a foeman worthy of his
steel, he esteemed the philosopher the more after
the combat of their wits.

Henry Giles, in his "Human Life of Shakespeare," calls Touchstone "The Hamlet of motley," and finds "a sadness in his jests" and "in his mockery seem(s) to hear echoes from a solitary heart." He epigrammatically summarizes the character as follows: "He is a thinker out of place, a philosopher in mistaken vesture, a genius by nature, an outcast by destiny." It may be presumption on my part to differ from so distinguished an authority, but, while I approve the application of the term "Hamlet of motley" as justified by Touchstone's analogy to the Danish prince in his reflective philosophy on the mutability of life, I fail to find any evidence of "sadness in his jests" or the "echoes from a solitary heart" in his sentiments or conduct. As I have before observed, his jests are not frivolous, but they are characteristic of the man, quaint and sententious, and never lacking in humor. On the arrival of the fool in the forest of Arden, with Celia and Rosalind, he jests at the love tale which he and the ladies overhear Sylvius relate to Corin, and burlesques the amatory verses that Orlando has written to Rosalind. He meets and courts Audrey, the country wench, with the usual attentions and compliments of a lover in his station, and in the third act arranges to marry her; in fact, he would have done so, but for the advice of Jaques, who urges him to postpone the ceremony till a more favorable opportunity. This opportunity presents itself at the conclusion of the play, and Touchstone is there with his sweetheart, eager, as he declares, to "swear and forswear, according as marriage binds." These conditions do not seem to indicate a solitary heart. As to Mr. Giles's final summary of Touchstone's character, his genius I admit; but a thinker is never out of place: there is no distinctive vesture for a philosopher: and the jester to so important a personage as the Duke can scarcely be termed an outcast.

It would seem by the initial appearance of Touchstone that Shakespeare intended to represent him as the ordinary type of "a dull fool," and later endowed him with the wealth of wit and wisdom that has so enriched the character, and made it so conspicuous in the comedy.

This has caused so eminent an authority as Dr. Furness to conclude that Shakespeare intended to present two separate and distinct characters: an ordinary "roynish clown" or "clownish fool," as he is called in the first act, and the keen and witty philosopher, the "worthy fool" we find in the later acts.

Again, I am compelled to differ with a distinguished scholar.

I can find nothing inconsistent in the character.

In the first act, Touchstone's jests are light and frivolous, but in perfect keeping with the duties of his office, which were to entertain and amuse his master and his household; and even that trifling example of the knight and the pancakes is an apt illustration of his argument on "swearing by his honor"; while his sarcastic reference to "breaking of ribs" as "sport for ladies" is entirely consistent with his philosophic satire in the later acts.

The unities of the character are well preserved, and the link connecting Touchstone at the court with Touchstone in the forest is clearly defined.

Rosalind and Celia, having decided to leave the court and seek security in the forest, Rosalind proposes:

> What if we assay'd to steal
> The clownish fool out of your father's court?
> Would he not be a comfort to our travel?

To this proposal Celia eagerly assents:

> He'll go along o'er the wide world with me;
> Leave me alone to woo him.

That her wooing was successful is obvious, for the next time we meet them they are at the edge of the forest, Touchstone is with them, and like themselves wearied by the journey they have made. The continuity is complete. The same trenchant wit that satirized the "breaking of ribs" at the court, humorously exclaims against the fatigues of the journey, and the discomforts of the forest.

Ros.   O Jupiter! how weary are my spirits!
Tou.   I care not for my spirits, if my legs were not weary.
Cel.   I pray you bear with me; I cannot go further.
Tou.   For my part, I had rather bear with you than

bear you; yet I should bear no cross if I did bear you,
for I think you have no money in your purse.

Ros. Well, this is the forest of Arden.

Tou. Ay, now I am in Arden; the more fool I!
when I was at home, I was in a better place: but
travelers must be content.

It is obvious to me that the characters developed
in the mind of the author as he progressed in the
construction of the play, and however clear may
have been his first conception of the part, he elaborated and perfected it as the possibilities presented themselves.

Dr. Furness, however, is most emphatic against
this view of Shakespeare's methods. He says:
"I cannot suppose—it is unthinkable—that from
the first instant each character was not present
before him in perfect symmetry and absolute completeness."

This is the natural point of view of such an accomplished scholar and scientific literary critic as
Dr. Furness; but Shakespeare had not the Doctor's
advantages of a systemized education, nor such
profound literary culture. Shakespeare adopted
methods of his own, which were at variance with

conventionality; he discarded the scientific rules of construction, followed the natural instincts of his own mind, and established a new standard of dramatic writing.

Such evidence as we have, indicates that nearly all of the poet's play-writing was hastily done, and as he then thought, but for temporary use on the stage.   We have no evidence of revision either for publication or for subsequent reproduction, but much that justifies the inference that he was indifferent to the merits of his dramatic work; so that while his plots may have been carefully prepared, the characters grew in detailed importance as they developed in the mind of the actor-dramatist, and the construction of the play proceeded.   It must also be remembered that Shakespeare worked from more than one point of view; he possessed the creative faculty of the author, the ideality of the poet, the constructive ability of the dramatist, as well as the actor's instinct of delineation.   This condition I assume to have existed in the construction of "As You Like It," and the result was the evolution of Touchstone.

The story of the knight and the pancakes, referred to in the foregoing lines, is told by Touchstone in the second scene of the first act; his initial
appearance in the play.

Rosalind and Celia are in the gardens of the
Duke's palace, when they are approached by
Touchstone, who addressing Celia, says:—"Mistress, you must come away to your father." Celia
responds with the question, "Were you made the
messenger?" "No, by mine honor," asserts
Touchstone, "but I was bid to come for you."
Honor being a quality with which a fool was not
supposed to be familiar, his asseveration draws
from Rosalind the query, "Where learned you that
oath, fool?" to which Touchstone replies as follows: "Of a certain knight who swore by his
honor they were good pancakes, and swore by his
honor the mustard was naught. Now I'll stand
to it, the pancakes were naught and the mustard was good, and yet was not the knight forsworn."

The ladies at this apparent trifling, grow sarcastic, Celia asking, "How prove you that in the

great heap of your knowledge?" Rosalind echoes her cousin's sentiment by adding, "Ay, marry, now unmuzzle your wisdom." For answer, Touchstone requests the ladies, "Stand you both forth now; stroke your chins, and swear by your beards that I am a knave." The ladies do as requested, passing their hands over their faces, Celia exclaiming, "By our beards, if we had them, thou art." Touchstone concludes the story and the argument by asserting: "By my knavery, if I had it, then I were; but if you swear by that that is not, you are not forsworn. No more was this knight, swearing by his honor, for he never had any; or if he had, he had sworn it away before ever he saw those pancakes or that mustard."

Learning from the fool that the story has reference to a friend of her father, Celia threatens him with the whip, for "taxation." Touchstone's reply is worthy of the keenest satirist: "The more pity, that fools may not speak wisely when wise men do foolishly."

The advent of Le Beau, a courtier, puts an end to the discussion. Le Beau invites the ladies to see some wrestling, which he terms "good sport," and describes with much detail the bouts that have already occurred, in which Charles, the champion wrestler, has overthrown and broken the ribs of three young men, brothers, who have essayed to compete with him. Le Beau reports the young men as having been apparently fatally injured, and that some of the more sympathetic spectators have joined the aged father of the boys in his lamentations at their hurts. At the conclusion of Le Beau's narrative Touchstone gravely inquires, "But what is the sport, Monsieur, that the ladies have lost?" "Why, this that I speak of," returns the courtier. "Thus," replies Touchstone, "men may grow wiser every day! It is the first time that ever I heard breaking of ribs was sport for ladies."

In the early days of my dramatic experience, there was an unworthy "gag" introduced into this scene by comedians who played Touchstone. At the conclusion of the wrestling, which is witnessed by the ladies and Touchstone, the champion is worsted by Orlando, and thrown senseless to the ground. The duke, with whom the wrestler is a favorite, inquires with some anxiety, "How dost thou, Charles?" in reply to which Le Beau should answer, "He cannot speak, my lord." Comedians, however, were permitted to appropriate this line and would preface it with the words, "He says," making the sentence in its entirety read, "He says he cannot speak, my lord!" a poverty-stricken jest of which Touchstone would have been incapable. Happily, this "gag" is now omitted.

The journey of Rosalind, Celia and Touchstone to the forest of Arden has been already referred to, together with the latter's witticisms on the subject, but there is one passage of the fool's I cannot refrain from repeating, "Travelers must be content."

Speaking from many years of experience over many miles and in many lands, I know of no bit of wisdom, wit, or philosophy in the realm of literature that expresses a more emphatic truth than those four words of Touchstone.

It is while resting "in the skirt of the forest"

that the travelers, unperceived, overhear a lover's complaint by a young shepherd, Sylvius, to his more mature friend Corin. The relation of the passion of the young shepherd brings from Rosalind the acknowledgment that she is similarly affected; and Touchstone declares he too has suffered, and humorously describes his experiences with Jane Smile, concluding with the sage averment: "We that are true lovers run into strange capers; but as all is mortal in nature, so is all nature in love mortal in folly." The sentiment is approved by Rosalind, who remarks, "Thou speakest wiser than thou art ware of." "Nay," modestly replies Touchstone, "I shall ne'er be ware of mine own wit till I break my shins against it"

Touchstone's adaptability and good nature soon make him friends and in the third act we find him in pleasant converse with the old shepherd Corin, who evidently has considerable respect for him, for he addresses him first as "Master Touchstone" and subsequently as "Sir." Corin's homely wit, however, is no match for that of

Touchstone, but the latter is compelled, in justice, to acknowledge that even in the limited sphere of his pastoral life the shrewd observations of the old shepherd have made him a natural philosopher. The dialogue is bright and characteristic throughout the scene, but the passages quoted below are especially good examples of Touchstone's logical reasoning.

Cor. And how like you this shepherd's life, Master Touchstone?

Tou. Truly, shepherd, in respect of itself, it is a good life; but in respect that it is a shepherd's life, it is naught. In respect that it is solitary, I like it very well; but in respect that it is private, it is a very vile life. Now, in respect it is in the fields, it pleaseth me well; but in respect it is not in the court, it is tedious. As it is a spare life, look you, it fits my humor well: but as there is no more plenty in it, it goes much against my stomach.—Wast ever at court, Shepherd?

Cor. No, truly.

Tou. Then thou art damned.

Cor. For not being at court? Your reason.

Tou. Why, if thou never wast at court, thou never saw'st good manners; if thou never saw'st good manners, then thy manners must be wicked; and wickedness is sin, and sin is damnation.

A little more reasoning, and Corin confesses himself unable to cope further with Touchstone:

Cor. You have too courtly a wit for me; I'll rest.
Tou. Wilt thou rest damned? God help thee, shallow man. If thou be'st not damned for this, the devil himself will have no shepherds.

It is evident that at this time Touchstone has not yet fallen a victim to the bucolic charms of Audrey; for he ridicules, with extemporaneous doggerel, the very interesting love verses that Rosalind has found hanging on the forest trees, and so seriously offends the lady that he is summarily dismissed from her presence.

Shortly after, however, in spite of his sad experience with Jane Smile, we find him paying assiduous court to the rustic maiden, Audrey; offering "to fetch up her goats," plying her with the usual questions, and awaiting her replies with the usual anxiety of a lover; but the court fool's language and references to classic Ovid are beyond the understanding of the simple country wench, who ingenuously asks for further information. This is somewhat discouraging to the motley lover, and he thus complains: "When a man's verses cannot be understood, nor a man's good wit seconded with the forward child Understanding, it strikes a man more dead than a great reckoning in a little room."

He then expresses the wish that the gods had made her poetical. This, too, is beyond Audrey's comprehension, and she artlessly inquires, "Is it honest in deed and word? Is it a true thing?" In spite of Touchstone's desire that Audrey should be poetical, he has apparently no very exalted opinion of poetry, for in reply to her query he replies, "No, truly, for the truest poetry is the most feigning; and lovers are given to poetry; and what they swear in poetry may be said as lovers they do feign."

I must confess that I find almost as much diffi-culty as Audrey in comprehending the argument of Touchstone in the following passages. To Audrey's query, "Do you wish then that the gods had made me poetical?" Touchstone replies, "I do, truly; for thou swear'st to me thou art honest: now, if thou wert a poet, I might have some hope thou didst feign." These words are clear enough, even to the simple understanding of Audrey, who asks in surprise, "Would you not have me honest?" It is Touchstone's reply to this question that I find confusing. He evidently has a sincere affection for this homely country girl; he admires her ingenuous simplicity in spite of her ignorance, and his intentions are honorable, for he proposes to make her his wife; yet he answers Audrey's question, first, with an emphatic negative, "No, truly," and then makes the following reservation, 'Unless thou wert hard favour'd," and gives the concluding illogical reason, "For honesty coupled to beauty is to have honey a sauce to sugar." It may be that Touchstone's worldly wisdom sees danger in too many virtues, and the honesty of Audrey is sufficient attraction without beauty. There is a ring of sincerity in Audrey's rejoinder; a note that argues well for harmony, and a longer voyage on the sea of matrimony than Jaques allots them. Audrey may not be learned or poetical, but neither is she shallow nor vain like the little shepherdess, Phoebe; she is not coquetting for a compliment, but with refreshing candor admits: "Well, I am not fair, and therefore I pray the gods to make me honest." I find in Audrey's simple prayer and womanly candor qualities indicating that in the choice of a wife Touchstone has neither been unwise nor unfortunate.

It would appear that Touchstone had little doubt of the success of his suit, for he not only tells Audrey that he will marry her, but has anticipated matters by engaging Sir Oliver Martext, the vicar of the next village, to meet them "in this place in the forest, and to couple us."

That Audrey approves of this hasty wooing is evidenced by her characteristically implied consent, "Well, the gods give us joy!" to which Touchstone adds, "Amen!"

As the fateful moment approaches, however, Touchstone indulges in some self-communion: "A man may, if he were of a fearful heart, stagger in this attempt; for here we have no temple but the wood, no assembly but horn-beasts. But what, though? . . . Is the single man therefore blessed? No; as a walled town is more worthier

than a village, so is the forehead of a married man
more honorable than the bare brow of a bachelor;
and by how much defense is better than no skill,
by so much is a horn more precious than to want."

Having arrived at this conclusion, Sir Oliver
Martext having arrived also, Touchstone is anx-
ous that the ceremony shall proceed, and asks of
the vicar, "Will you despatch us here under the
tree, or shall we go with you to your chapel?"
For reply, the vicar, looking around, asks, "Is
there none here to give the woman?" to which the
fool, who is obviously unfamiliar with the marriage service responds, "I will not take her on gift
of any man." As this attitude of Touchstone
seems liable to postpone indefinitely, if not prevent
the ceremony altogether, Jaques, who has been lis-
tening unobserved to the entire scene, steps forward and offers his services. Having, however,
acquired a profound respect for Touchstone, and
perceiving that he is in earnest in his desire to be
married to Audrey, Jaques urges him to have the
ceremony performed in a church by a properly or-
dained minister, and the appropriate surroundings

of a gentleman; rather than by a hedge-priest in the forest, like a beggar. Touchstone hesitates before adopting this course, and Shakespeare has put an aside speech into his mouth, which if taken seriously would destroy much of our respect for him. Some of the commentators have taken it seriously, and have deduced the conclusion that Touchstone intended to deceive Audrey; but I cannot think it. Every action of the fool, and every other line that the author has given him, expresses sincere regard and indicates honorable intentions. The entire speech seems to me to be the spontaneous expression of the humor of the situation, as it appears to the keen sense of our motley friend. The subject matter is not new nor the treatment of it original. Marriage has been the theme of jest at all times, to all conditions of people, and Touchstone was too instinctively a jester not to appreciate the possibility of a jest, even on himself. The lines are as follows: (Aside) "I am not in the mind but I were better to be married of him than of another, for he is not like to marry me well, and not being well

married, will be a good excuse for me hereafter
to leave my wife."

However, Touchstone and Audrey accompany
Jaques to discuss the matter further, leaving the
despised Sir Oliver in high dudgeon, and without
a fee.

Jaques evidently succeeded in convincing
Touchstone of the propriety of his suggestion, but
Audrey fails to comprehend the necessity of delay.   To her limited understanding, one priest is
as good as another.   In the first scene of the fifth
act she emphatically expresses her impatience, indicating that she has an opinion, if not a will, of
her own, and protests, "Faith, the priest was good
enough, for all the old gentleman's saying."
Touchstone finds it quite a task for his wit to
pacify the lady, and is only successful by diverting her attention to the claims of another to her
affections; a certain forest youth named William.
It is a shrewd piece of diplomacy on the part of
the fool, and not new to the world by any means;
to terminate an argument by changing the subject, and affecting reproach, or of meeting one

accusation by making another.   Audrey, however, denies the soft impeachment, and fortunately the bucolic gentleman referred to appears most opportunely on the scene.

Touchstone regards the newcomer critically, and complacently observes, "It is meat and drink to me to see a clown.   By my troth, we that have good wits have much to answer for; we shall be flouting, we cannot hold."

It is a curiously contrasted group we have before us now: The country girl, awkward and embarrassed in the presence of her rustic suitor, and her court trained lover; the forest youth, ill at ease, nervously shifting from one foot to the other, as he stands, hat in hand before her; and the smug, self-satisfied court fool, who conscious of possession, revels in his superiority, and rejoices in the discomfiture of his unsuccessful rival.

With what a delightful assumption of patronage, Touchstone questions the simple William, encourages, emboldens, then confuses, and finally drives the poor fellow from the field with the most terrible threats of disaster and death.   The scene is rich in comedy, but beneath the surface may be appreciated a deep satire on the world.

One passage especially, presents a most wholesome truth, that it is superfluous for me to emphasize, but which I cannot forbear quoting. Amongst other questions, Touchstone asks of William, "Art thou wise?" William incautiously replies, "Ay, sir, I have a pretty wit." This is Touchstone's opportunity, and he retorts: "Why, thou sayest well. I do now remember a saying, The fool doth think he is wise, but the wise man knows himself to be a fool."

Touchstone is now summoned by his "master and mistress" (Rosalind, disguised as Ganymede, and Celia), who evidently acquaint him of their matrimonial intentions, and approve of his; for the next time we meet the motley "lover and his lass," the former tells her, "To-morrow is the joyful day, Audrey; to-morrow will we be married," to which she candidly and sensibly replies, "I do desire it with all my heart; and I hope it is no dishonest desire to be a woman of the world."

Audrey's wishes are shortly realized; Rosalind,

the good fairy, waves her wand, and the forest of Arden becomes a veritable Temple of Hymen. All differences are adjusted, all wrongs righted, and true love receives its reward. It is a joyous meeting of their betters, to which Touchstone brings his prospective bride, and to which they are heralded by Jaques in his characteristic fashion: "There is, sure, another flood toward, and these couples are coming to the ark! Here comes a pair of very strange beasts, which in all tongues are called fools."

However, on their appearance he bespeaks a welcome for them from the Duke: "Good my lord, like this fellow," to which the Duke courteously replies, "I like him very well."

Touchstone's acknowledgment is characteristic, if not especially gallant; but his self-abnegation is scarcely consistent with his previously expressed declaration, that he would not take Audrey "on gift of any man." However, his concluding epigram is convincing, and his metaphor perfect: "God 'ield you, sir! I desire of you the like. I press in here, sir, amongst the rest of the country copulatives, to swear and forswear, according as marriage binds and blood breaks. A poor virgin, sir, an ill-favored thing, sir, but mine own; a poor humor of mine, sir, to take that that no man else will. Rich honesty dwells like a miser, sir, in a poor house, as your pearl in your foul oyster."

The completeness of the character of Touchstone is achieved in his last scene, which I have given below in full, with some slight transpositions. Here Touchstone is in his element. Surrounded by persons who understand his office and can appreciate his wit, he appears at his best. The various accomplishments by which he claims the title of a courtier, are irresistibly amusing, and the humor may be applied to some modern views on gallantry, as well as to mediæval standards of courtesy.

No less entertaining is Touchstone's parody on certain books on good manners, and on the ethics of honor, which attracted some attention at this time; and there is a vein of the most delicious satire in his definitions of the degrees of a lie, the cause of a quarrel, and the efficacy of that redeeming, and peace-restoring preposition "if."

Jaques' presentation of Touchstone to the Duke, and the subsequent dialogue is as follows:

Jaq.   Good my lord, bid him welcome. This is the motley-minded gentleman that I have so often met in the forest; he hath been a courtier, he swears.

Tou.   If any man doubt that, let him put me to my purgation. I have trod a measure; I have flattered a lady; I have been politic with my friend, smooth with mine enemy; I have undone three tailors; I have had four quarrels, and like to have fought one.

Jaq.   And how was that ta'en up?

Tou.   Faith, we met and found the quarrel was upon the seventh cause.

Jaq.   How did you find the quarrel on the seventh cause?

Tou.   Upon a lie seven times removed—as thus, sir. I did dislike the cut of a certain courtier's beard. He sent me word, if I said his beard was not cut well, he was in the mind it was: this is called the Retort Courteous. If I sent him word again it was not well cut, he would send me word he cut it to please himself, this is called the Quip Modest. If again, it was not well cut, he disabled my judgment; this is called the Reply Churlish. If again it was not well cut, he would answer, I spake not true; this is called the Reproof Valiant. If again, it was not well cut, he would say I lied; this is called the Countercheck

Quarrelsome: and so to the Lie Circumstantial and
the Lie Direct.

Jaq. And how oft did you say his beard was not
well cut?

Tou. I durst go no further than the Lie Circumstantial, nor he durst not give me the Lie Direct; and
so we measured swords and parted.

Jaq. Can you nominate in order now the degrees
of a lie?

Tou. O sir, we quarrel in print by the book, as
you have books for good manners. I will name you
the degrees: the first, the Retort Courteous; the second, the Quip Modest; the third, the Reply Churlish;
the fourth, the Reproof Valiant; the fifth, the Countercheck Quarrelsome; the sixth, the Lie with Circumstance; the seventh, the Lie Direct. All these you
may avoid but the Lie Direct; and you may avoid that
too, with an 'If'! I knew when seven justices could
not take up a quarrel, but when the parties were met
themselves, one of them thought but of an if! as, "If
you said so, then I said so;" and they shook hands
and swore brothers. Your "if" is the only peace-
maker; much virtue in "If."

The concluding compliment of Jaques is but a
just tribute to the accomplishments of Touchstone, and well epitomizes what I conceive to be
the poet's conception; while the reply of the Duke
indicates the vein of satirical truth that underlies

the entire character, and summarizes the motive, as well as the result of the author's clearly expressed intention.

Jaq. Is not this a rare fellow, my lord? he's as good at anything, and yet a fool.
Duke. He uses his folly like a stalking horse, and under the presentation of that he shoots his wit.

It was my privilege to take part in the great dramatic festival held in Cincinnati, in 1885. One of the plays produced was "As You Like It." I played the part of Orlando to the Rosalind of that fine actress, Fanny Davenport. Stuart Robson was the Touchstone of the occasion, and I recall with pleasure the unique and interesting performance he gave of the character. His dress was that of the conventional jesters; parti-colored doublet and hose of the period, with the traditional hood, cockscomb and bauble. His walk, or perhaps I could better describe it as a strut, was like that of the barnyard bird whose head adorned his own, and his carriage was in harmony with the same idea. His voice: what playgoer who has once seen and heard Stuart Robson in any of his humorous characters can forget that voice! The peculiar lisp with its ever changing nflections, rising to a high treble at the end of each sentence, accompanied with a constant snapping of the eyes, and an abrupt jerking of the head from side to side, at almost every other word.

Mr. Robson was held in high esteem so that his appearance was greeted with hearty applause, and almost every phrase he uttered, with roars of laughter. The story of the knight and the pancakes never seemed to me so humorous, while the request to Celia and Rosalind, to "stand forth, stroke your chins and swear by your beards, etc." was so ludicrous that the ladies themselves were convulsed with laughter and scarcely able to proceed with their lines.

Another scene in which Mr. Robson appeared to the greatest advantage was in Scene I of the Fifth Act; located in the forest of Arden. The characters are Touchstone, Audrey, his country sweetheart, and William, a simple rustic. The latter character, though comparatively unimpor-

tant, was on this occasion played by Mr. William
H. Crane, out of compliment to his old friend
and comrade Mr. Robson, with whom he had
been so long associated.   The delightful air of
superiority assumed by the court fool over the
bucolic youth, who in his smock frock stood with
vacuous stare and open-mouthed wonder in fearful awe of his motley tormentor, was a splendid
contrast of diversified humor.   The keen, incisive
quality of Mr. Robson's comedy and the intelligent understanding and appreciation of the text
underlying it was never better exampled than
by his delivery of that potent truism, "The fool
doth think he is wise, but the wise man knows
himself to be a fool."   It was indeed, a gem of
wisdom in a setting of golden comedy.   Again,
the assumption of anger, the direful threats of
bloodthirsty consequences with which he over-
whelmed the terror-stricken William and drove
him from the field, leaving the fool in full and
undisputed possession of his lady love were simply
delicious.

This scene was rendered doubly effective by the

skill and sincerity with which Mr. Crane played the part of William. Like a true artist, he gave this small bit of character work the same attention to every detail as though it were the principal part in the comedy. In appearance, he looked as if he had stepped out of an old English engraving of rural life; his dialect was perfect and his ungainly walk and awkward bearing reminded one of the types that may yet be seen and heard in the remote villages of the midland counties in England.

In spite of Mr. Robson's success in the earlier scenes of the play, I think he was most effective in the last act. It may be remembered that here the various threads of the plot are drawn together and the fabric of the story completed. After their adventures in the forest, the several couples, by mutual arrangement, meet at a certain point where their differences are arranged, their misunderstandings explained and their conciliations effected. Among them, come Touchstone and Audrey. Here Robson fairly reveled in the situation. He strutted, he crowed, and to continue the simile, he flapped his wings with the triumphant satisfaction of a barnyard rooster; argued his right to be called a courtier with the logic of a lawyer, and expounded the degrees of a lie with the wisdom of an oracle.

What old playgoer does not recall the delicacy and refinement of Mr. James Lewis's performance of the Shakespearean clowns in the several comedy revivals at Daly's Theater, New York. "As You Like It" was produced there in the early eighties, with Ada Rehan as Rosalind, John Drew as Orlando, and Mr. Lewis (Little Jimmie Lewis, as he was affectionately called) as Touchstone. The cameo clearness of his conception, the quaint incisiveness of his delivery, the significance of his business, and the delicate finish of the entire characterization left an impression never to be forgotten. The performance had not that breadth of humor given to it by some comedians, nor the rich unction of others, but it was imbued with the quaint little gentleman's own personal-

ity, and presented with an artistic instinct that
permeated every character he assumed.

I was a witness to an eloquent though silent
tribute paid to Mr. Lewis by a stranger, of which
the actor was, at the time, unconscious.

Mr. Lewis was walking down Broadway one
afternoon in the early fall. I was a short distance behind him. Approaching, somewhat
slowly, from the opposite direction was a well-
groomed gentleman of middle age, apparently a
business man returning from his office down town.
The expression of the gentleman was absorbed
and thoughtful, as if he were revolving some
knotty problem in his mind. As he neared Mr.
Lewis he raised his eyes and, recognizing the
comedian, his expression changed completely; a
smile replaced his frown, his eyes brightened, and
the careworn look left him entirely. He paused
slightly as Mr. Lewis passed him, looked after
the retreating figure of the comedian a second,
then resumed his journey up town with a quick-

ened step and smiling face, the tenor of his thoughts apparently changed and brightened by the memory of the pleasures he had enjoyed by the performances of the talented little gentleman he had so unexpectedly met and recognized.

I related the incident to Mr. Lewis later. It gratified him exceedingly, and he told me he felt it to be one of the most delightful compliments he had ever received.

Another Touchstone worthy of note was that presented by Mr. Edwin Stevens, the successor of Mr. Lewis as the comedian of Daly's Theater. Equally artistic was Mr. Stevens, but entirely different in methods as he was in features and physique. Mr. Stevens seemed to take his position more seriously than Mr. Lewis and maintained a greater personal dignity. He spoke his lines with the deliberation of oracular wisdom rather than with spontaneous wit, and among the courtiers carried himself as a social equal rather than as a retainer. He wooed the humble Audrey with condescension, and accepted commendation as a matter of course. It was a most delightful performance of the character from the point of view of Mr. Stevens, and a worthy achievement of a versatile and intelligent artist.

TRINCULO

IN

THE TEMPEST

"What a pied ninny's this."

TRINCULO, in "The Tempest," is the only one of Shakespeare's fools who in the dramatis personæ of the play is called a jester; and is the one least worthy of the title.

Fool to the court of Alonzo, King of Naples, Trinculo, while accompanying his master and others on a sea voyage, is shipwrecked and cast, with them, upon an unknown and apparently uninhabited island. Here he has wonderful adventures, meets extraordinary beings, and is brought, by the art of Prospero, the genius of the island, under the influence of fairies, sprites, goblins, and other strange creatures of the author's imagination.

Whatever may have been Trinculo's ability as

a wit at court, he certainly does not appear to great advantage in that respect on the island, although, it must be admitted, he is environed by an atmosphere of discomfort and danger, which while affording amusement to the observer, savors little of humor to him.

In his first scene he is out on an open plain, "with neither bush nor shrub" in a heavy storm; on his next appearance he is under the influence of liquor; and the third time we meet him, he has been pursued by fiends through a horse-pond, and is saturated with its offensive contents.

He is dominated in the first instance by terror, in the second by liquor, in the third by anger and disgust; and is in turn cowardly, maudlin, silly and disgusting. His wit is the poorest kind of punning, and his pranks, if so they may be called, are not spontaneous fun, but drunken folly.

He is ungrateful and treacherous. On being rescued from the sea, he exhibits no anxiety for the safety of his master, nor loyalty to his memory, when he is supposed to be lost; and he readily joins in the miserable plot with Stephano, the drunken butler, to murder Prospero, and gain possession of the island.

Even Caliban, the ignorant semi-savage, has a contempt for him, and in turn calls him "a pied ninny," "a jesting monkey," and "a scurvy patch"; while Stephano, his countryman and comrade, in reply to the fool's boast that "I can swim like a duck," retorts, "Though thou cans't swim like a duck, thou art made like a goose"; and does not hesitate to strike him when he is offended.

The most pointed epigram made by Trinculo is in the second scene of the second act, when, seeking shelter from the storm under the gaberdine of Caliban, who is apparently dead, he says, "Misery acquaints a man with strange bedfellows."

His best retort is in the last scene of the last act, while still enveloped in the foul effluvium of the horse-pond, when he is asked by Alonzo, his master, "How cam'st thou in this pickle?" to which he replies: "I have been in such a pickle,

T. C. Cooke as "Trinculo" in "The Tempest"

since I saw you last, that, I fear me, will never out of my bones; I shall not fear fly-blowing."

He indicates no learning, and his philosophy is superficial. Of this he is apparently conscious, for in Act three, Scene two, he says: "There's but five upon this isle; we are three of them; if the other two be brained like us, the state totters."

As to his courage, it is best described by himself: "Was there ever man a coward, that hath drunk so much sack as I to-day?"

Taken in its entirety, I cannot but regard the character of Trinculo as the least interesting of the court jesters that Shakespeare has given us; a character type that was still in existence when the poet lived and wrote, examples of which he must have seen at Kenilworth, at the court of Elizabeth, and later at that of James I, in London. The species, however, was rapidly becoming extinct; printing began to develop, knowledge to be more general, and literature to be appreciated; entertainment was found in the printed publications of wit and humor, rather than from the lips of the jester, and the quality of the latter began to deteriorate from the witty retainer of the court, to the coarse buffoon whose jests appealed to the low and the ignorant, rather than to the cultivated and intelligent.

It was at this period of deterioration that Shakespeare wrote "The Tempest," and possibly his conception of Trinculo may be based upon the conditions that then existed, and the character made to present his own view of the coarseness of expression and the poverty of wit exhibited by the professional fools of his time.

That Shakespeare was alive to the current events of the period in which he wrote is illustrated by a passage spoken by Trinculo in his first scene.

A number of American Indians had been brought from the newly established colony of Virginia to London; the novelty of their color, appearance and dress attracted great attention, and caused considerable excitement and curiosity. One of the Indians succumbed to the rigors of the

English climate, and died, the corpse being subsequently placed on public exhibition, many persons paying a substantial fee to look at it.

When Trinculo sees the apparently dead body of Caliban lying upon the ground, and does not know whether it is "a man or a fish," but from its foul odor believes it to be the latter, the poet satirizes the prevailing sensation, in the words of the fool: "A strange fish! Were I in England now (as I once was) and had but this fish painted, not a holiday fool there but would give a piece of silver; there would this monster make a man; any strange beast there makes a man. When they will not give a doit to relieve a lame beggar, they will lay out ten to see a dead Indian."

FESTE

IN

TWELFTH NIGHT

*"I am indeed not her fool, but her corrupter of
words"*

IN the list of the characters in "Twelfth
Night," the fool is not given a name. He is
coupled with Fabian, as "Clown," and together
they are called "Servants to Olivia," but in Act
2, Scene 4 of the play, he is spoken of by Curio,
a gentleman attending on the Duke, as "Feste,"
and is described as "the jester, a fool that the
Lady Olivia's father took much delight in." He
is a combination of jester and minstrel, and is a
member of the household of the Countess Olivia,
a wealthy noblewoman of Illyria.

Feste is not of the gentle disposition of Yorick,
nor of the mental fiber of Touchstone; his wit has
neither the spontaneous humor we can imagine in

the former, nor the sententious wisdom we find in the latter; it is at times labored, frequently forced, and seldom free from obvious effort. It is professional foolery, rather than intuitive fun.

He is o' the world, worldly; his conversation is coarse, even for the period, and many of his jests are vulgar.

His retorts are neither keen nor incisive; they have the brutality of the cudgel, rather than the point of the rapier.

He trusts more to "good fooling" than to ready wit, and many of his sallies are but thinly disguised impudence; yet it must be admitted that at times he makes some telling points, and delivers some very clever epigrams.

He is shrewd and thrifty if not covetous; he does not scruple to accept money, even from strangers, nor does he hesitate broadly to suggest liberality to those patrons who are tardy with their bounty.

Disguised as Sir Topaz he quotes Latin aptly and accurately; he shows familiarity with Gre-

cian history and legend, and is not unacquainted
with the philosophy of Pythagoras.

In spite of his knowledge, he appears to be tolerated rather than appreciated; and although he
is admitted to the revels of Sir Toby Belch, and
Sir Andrew Aguecheek, on a comparative equality, it is chiefly on account of his accomplishments
as a minstrel. He associates with the servants
of the house, and is treated as one by his mistress.

His best friend appears to be Maria, the wait-
ing-woman to Lady Olivia. On his first appearance in the play, in Act 1, Scene 5, he is apparently seeking her good offices with her mistress,
to excuse his evidently unauthorized, and lengthy
absence from the household. With feminine
curiosity Maria endeavors to gain from him an
account of his truancy, but Feste shrewdly avoids
any compromising admissions. Maria, somewhat
irritated, expresses herself with characteristic decision, and warns him of the severe punishment
he may expect. Feste assumes a recklessness, but
realizes the gravity of his offense:

Mar. Nay, either tell me where thou hast been, or I will not open my lips so wide as a bristle may enter in way of thy excuse; my lady will hang thee for thy absence.

Clo. Let her hang me; he that is well hanged in this world needs to fear no colors.

Mar. Make that good.

Clo. He shall see none to fear.

Mar. A good lenten answer; I can tell thee where that saying was born, of "I fear no colors."

Clo. Where, good Mistress Mary?

Mar. In the wars; and that may you be bold to say in your foolery.

Clo. Well, God give them wisdom that have it; and those that are fools, let them use their talents.

Mar. Yet you will be hanged for being so long absent. . . . Here comes my lady; make your excuse wisely, you were best.

Maria leaves him, and being alone Feste thus soliloquizes: "Wit, an't be thy will, put me into good fooling! Those wits, that think they have thee, do very oft prove fools; and I, that am sure I lack thee, may pass for a wise man; for what says Quinapalus? 'Better a witty fool than a foolish wit.'"

The Lady Olivia enters, whom he respectfully salutes, with: "God bless thee, lady!"

But the lady is evidently much displeased, and very promptly and indignantly commands: "Take the fool away."

With characteristic audacity the fool challenges the lady, in the following dialogue:

Clo. Do you not hear, fellows? Take away the lady.

Oli. Go to, you're a dry fool; I'll no more of you; besides you grow dishonest.

Clo. Two faults, madonna, that drink and good counsel will amend: for give the dry fool drink, then is the fool not dry; bid the dishonest man mend himself; if he mend, he is no longer dishonest; anything that's mended is but patched; virtue that transgresses is but patched with sin; and sin that amends is but patched with virtue. . . . The lady bade take away the fool; therefore I say again, take her away.

Oli. Sir, I bade them take away you.

Clo. Misprison in the highest degree! . . . Good madonna, give me leave to prove you a fool.

Oli. Can you do it?

Clo. Dexterously, good madonna.

Oli. Make your proof.

Clo. I must catechise you for it. . . . Good madonna, why mourn'st thou?

Oli. Good fool, for my brother's death.

Clo. I think his soul is in hell, madonna.

Oli. I know his soul is in heaven, fool.

Clo. The more fool, madonna, to mourn for your brother's soul being in heaven.—Take away the fool, gentlemen.

The wit of the fool somewhat molifies the anger of the lady, who appeals to Malvolio to endorse her approval of his readiness: "Doth he not mend?"

But the steward is no friend of Feste, and replies with a sarcasm that is not lost on the fool: "Yes; infirmity, that decays the wise, doth ever make the better fool."

This brings from Feste the prompt and clever retort: "God send you, sir, a speedy infirmity, for the better increasing your folly! Sir Toby will be sworn that I am no fox, but he will not pass his word for twopence that you are no fool."

Malvolio, thus goaded, continues to dispraise the fool, but Olivia warmly defends him, and administers a severe reproof to the steward for his vanity: "O, you are sick of self-love, Malvolio. . . . There is no slander in an allowed fool, though he do nothing but rail; nor no railing in a known discreet man, though he do nothing but reprove.''

Feste is not without gratitude to his mistress for his defense, and thus expresses it: ''Now Mercury endue thee with leasing, for thou speakest well of fools.''

But on the retirement of Malvolio, the lady does not hesitate to rebuke the fool: ''Now you see, sir, how your fooling grows old, and people dislike it.''

The dialogue is here interrupted by the advent of Sir Toby Belch, a cousin of the Lady Olivia, who appears on the scene in a very drunken condition. The lady is properly indignant, and demands of Feste: ''What's a drunken man like, fool?''

Feste replies: ''Like a drown'd man, a fool and a madman; one draught above heat makes him a fool, the second mads him, and a third drowns him.''

Olivia, pleased with the fool's epigrammatic humor, continues the pleasantry: ''Go thou and

seek the crowner, and let him sit o' my coz; for
he's in the third degree of drink, he's drowned:
go look after him."

Feste obeys, and retires with the words: "He
is but mad yet, madonna; and the fool shall look
to the madman."

In Marie Wainwright's production of this exquisite comedy, in which she toured the country
some seasons ago, the part of Feste was played
by Mr. E. Y. Bachus, who brought a keen intelligence and appreciation to his performance. In
the foregoing scene, Mr. Bachus mitigated the
gross impertinence of Feste to his mistress by the
introduction of some business that I believe was
entirely original with him. He carried in his
pouch or pocket some little dolls in the form of
diminutive zanies, which as the dialogue progressed he proceeded with apparent unconscious-
ness to dress. This business seemed to dull the
edge of his rudeness by dividing the attention of
his hearers between his words and his actions.
At the conclusion of the dialogue, Feste dropped

his little zanies on the ground; and at his exit Marie picked them up, and contemptuously threw them after him.

Feste next appears in the third scene of Act 2, joining in the noisy midnight revels of Sir Toby and Sir Andrew Aguecheek.   He sings them a love song, and without any special wit ridicules the shallow egotistical affectations of the one, and the drunken folly of the other.   He improvises a "catch" cleverly, but promptly disappears at the first sign of trouble.

Feste's ability as a minstrel is evidently known and appreciated, for in the fourth scene he is sent for by the Duke Orsino, to sing to him, who, at the conclusion of the song gives him money:

Duke.   There's for thy pains.
Fes.   No pains, sir; I take pleasure in singing, sir.
Duke.   I'll pay thy pleasure then.
Fes.   Truly, sir, and pleasure will be paid, one time or another.

A truism, as wise as witty.

The character as well as the compass of Feste's capacity is well illustrated in the first scene of the

third act, Olivia's garden. The fool, carrying
his tabor, is met by Viola, disguised as Cesario and
in an admirable interchange of equivoque aptly
describes the faculty of wit, the province of the
fool, and the prevalence of folly. The scene is
brief, but as a "corrupter of words" the fool appears to better advantage than in any other part of
the play, and displays a readiness of retort that is
not always in evidence. Viola furnishes him his
first opportunity by her greeting:

Vio. Save thee, friend, and thy music; dost thou
live by thy tabor?

Fes. No, sir, I live by the church.

Vio. Art thou a churchman?

Fes. No such matter, sir; I do live by the church;
for I do live at my house, and my house doth stand by
the church.

Vio. So thou may'st say the King lives by a beggar, if a beggar dwell near him; or, the church stands
by thy tabor, if thy tabor stand by the church.

Fes. You have said, sir. . . . A sentence is but a
cheveril glove to a good wit; how quickly the wrong
side may be turned outward!

Laughingly acknowledging the truth of this,
Viola compliments him on his humor and clever-

ness: "I warrant thou art a merry fellow, and carest for nothing."

The reply she receives, however, is neither polite nor encouraging: "Not so, sir, I do care for something; but in my conscience, sir, I do not care for you; if that be to care for nothing, sir, I would it would make you invisible."

Ignoring this discourtesy, Viola asks: "Art not thou the Lady Olivia's fool?"

Again Feste justifies his office by the description he gives of himself: "No, indeed, sir; the Lady Olivia has no folly; she will keep no fool, sir, till she be married; and fools are as like husbands as pilchards are to herrings; the husband's the bigger. I am indeed not her fool, but her corrupter of words."

In reply to Viola's assertion that she saw Feste recently at the palace of the Count Orsino, the jester gives us the following terse but eloquent truism: "Foolery, sir, doth walk about the orb like the sun; it shines everywhere."

At this, Viola, who is disguised as a youth, and is mistaken for one by Feste, offers him a coin.

In way of thanks the latter exclaims: "Now
Jove, in his next commodity of hair, send thee a
beard."

Viola is deeply in love with the Duke Orsino,
who is ignorant of her passion; and at this sally
of the fool, wittily rejoins: "By my troth, I'll
tell thee; I am almost sick for one, though I would
not have it grow on my chin."

Feste does not understand this allusion, but
holding the coin he has received in his hand,
makes the pointed suggestion: "Would not a
pair of these have bred, sir?"

Viola replies: "Yes, being kept together and
put to use."

Feste is resourceful, and returns to the charge
armed with a simile from Grecian legend.

Fes. I would play Lord Pandarus of Phrygia, sir,
to bring a Cressida to this Troilus.
Vio. I understand you, sir, 'tis well begged.
Fes. The matter, I hope, is not great, sir, begging
but a beggar; Cressida was a beggar.

Finding his efforts to increase his bounty inef-
fectual, Feste continues to "dally nicely with

words," and then retires. "My lady is within, sir. I will construe to them whence you come; who you are and what you would are out of my welkin; I might say element, but the word is overworn."

It is the preceding scene that suggests to Viola the passage that so aptly describes the requirements of a fool, which I have quoted at length in the introduction to this book, and which I reproduce here to accentuate its significance.

> This fellow's wise enough to play the fool;
> And to do that well craves a kind of wit;
> He must observe their mood on whom he jests,
> The quality of persons, and the time,
> And, like the haggard, check at every feather
> That comes before his eye. This is a practice
> As full of labor as a wise man's art;
> For folly that he wisely shows is fit;
> But wise men, folly-fallen, quite taint their wit.

The complications that arise in Act 4, consequent on the disguise of Viola as Cesario, and her subsequent mistaken identity for Sebastian, occur in rapid succession. Feste, of course, becomes involved in them, and in the first scene,

with the real Sebastian, there is a dialogue of
considerable humor. Feste, as usual, is "dal-
lying with words" and unusually, exhibiting some
impatience; however the irritation is quickly
allayed by the soothing application of a coin, a
remedy that seems effective with the fool at all
times.

In the second scene, Feste, at the instigation of
Maria, assumes the character of Sir Topaz, the
curate, to assist in tormenting his old enemy Malvolio, who, by a trick of that mischief-loving
maid, has been seized as a madman, bound, and
-confined in a dark cellar. The scene is one of
good fooling, rather than witty dialogue; but in
assuming the robe of the curate, Feste makes some
reflections indicating that sanctimony and hypoc-
risy were as prevalent in the days of Shakespeare
as they unfortunately are in ours:

Fes. Well I'll put it on, and I will dissemble myself in't, and I would I were the first that ever dis-
sembled in such a gown. I am not tall enough to become the function well, nor lean enough to be
thought a good student; . . . but as the old hermit of
Prague very wittily said to a niece of King Gorboduc,

"That that is, is; so I, being master parson, am master parson, for what is 'that' but 'that'? and 'is' but 'is'?"

He greets Sir Toby with a Latin salutation, and bears himself with humorous gravity as Sir Topaz. He uses big words, and applies them with a contrary meaning. He questions Malvolio as to his views on the opinions of Pythagoras concerning wild fowl, and leaves him with assumed indignation when the alleged lunatic will not agree with the philosopher.

Fes. Remain thou still in darkness. Thou shalt hold the opinion of Pythagoras, ere I will allow of thy wits, and fear to kill a woodcock, lest thou dispossess the soul of thy grandam.

Feste then doffs his disguise, and addresses Malvolio in his own character, with assumed sympathy: "Alas, sir, how fell you besides your five wits?"

"I am as well in my wits, fool, as thou art," replies Malvolio.

"Then," retorts Feste; "you are mad indeed, if you be no better in your wits than a fool."

Feste continues to plague the poor steward, now as Sir Topaz, now as himself, reveling in the prisoner's discomfiture till the man is almost distracted, and begs for candle, ink, and paper that he may communicate with his mistress. These articles Feste promises to obtain, but before going delivers a parting shaft:

Fes. Are you not mad indeed? or do you but counterfeit?

Mal. Believe me, I am not; I tell thee true.

Fes. Nay, I'll ne'er believe a madman till I see his brains.

And with a merry catch, the laughing fool leaves the poor imprisoned steward to his misery.

Malvolio evidently obtains his ink and paper, writes his letter, and intrusts it to Feste for delivery; the latter, however, pockets the missive, and on the principle that "A mad man's epistles are no gospels, so it skills not when they are delivered," keeps it there 'till inclination prompts, and opportunity provides a suitable occasion to present it to his mistress.

In the meantime, in company with Fabian, Feste

encounters the Duke Orsino, for whom he lately
sang. The Duke asks if they belong to the
household of the Lady Olivia. With his usual
effrontery and lack of reverence, he answers,
"Ay, sir, we are some of her trappings."

The Duke recognizes him, and graciously inquires: "How dost thou, my good fellow?"

His reply and argument are worthy a wiser
man than Feste, and exhibit a philosophy as
sound, as it is wholesome.

Fes. Truly, sir, the better for my foes and the
worse for my friends.
Duke. Just the contrary; the better for thy
friends.
Fes. No, sir, the worse.
Duke. How can that be?
Fes. Marry, sir, they praise me and make an ass
of me; now my foes tell me plainly I am an ass; so
that by my foes, sir, I profit in the knowledge of myself, and by my friends I am abused: . . . why, then,
the worse for my friends, and the better for my foes.

Appreciating the shrewd wisdom of the fool,
the Duke exclaims, "This is excellent," which
gives Feste an opportunity for one of the cleverest
retorts in the play:

Fes. By my troth, sir, no; though it please you to be one of my friends.

The Duke is himself not without wit, and promptly recognizing the ready sarcasm of the fool, replies: "Thou shalt not be the worse for me; there's gold."

Feste accepts the gratuity, and again exhibits his avaricious shrewdness by suggesting:

Fes. But that it would be double dealing, sir, I would you could make it another.

After a brief passage of protest and replication, the Duke yields to the fool's clever pleading:

Duke. Well, I will be so much a sinner to be a double-dealer; there's another.

Even this liberality does not satisfy the greed of the fool, who again importunes the Duke, on the principle that "The third pays for all." But that nobleman is not so easily cajoled, and delivers his ultimatum with some emphasis.

Duke. You can fool no more money out of me at this throw; if you will let your lady know I am here to speak with her, it may awake my bounty further.

Finding that any further effort to enlarge his purse at the expense of the Duke would be useless, for the present, Feste retires; not, however, without a parting hint of future possibilities.

Fes. Marry, sir, lullaby to your bounty till I come again. I go sir; but, as you say, sir, let your bounty take a nap, I will awake it anon.

After much delay, Feste finds an opportunity to deliver the letter of Malvolio to his mistress. She commands him to "open and read it," which he proceeds to do, prefacing his task with the admonition:

Fes. Look, then, to be well edified when the fool delivers the madman.

But Lady Olivia has had enough of his folly, and instructs another to read the letter, which being done explains the trick that has been played on Malvolio, and assists in unraveling the complications, and clearing up the mysteries of the play. Malvolio's humiliation is sufficient punishment to all but the fool, whose petty nature cannot refrain from gloating over his fallen foe, by repeating the passages in the decoying letter,

E. Y. Backus as "Feste" in "Twelfth Night"

and former reproaches that he has received at the hands of the steward:

Fes. Why, "Some are born great, some achieve greatness, and some have greatness thrown upon them," I was one, sir, in this interlude; . . . "By the Lord, fool, I am not mad." But do you remember? "Madam, why laugh you at such a barren rascal? an you smile not, he's gagged."

And to quote Feste's own words in conclusion: 'And thus the whirligig of time brings in his revenges."

At the culmination of what may be termed the serious interest of the play, all the characters except the clown retire: he being alone concludes the comedy with a song:

When that I was and a little tiny boy,
With hey, ho, the wind and the rain,
A foolish thing was but a toy,
For the rain it raineth every day.

But when I came to man's estate,
With hey, ho, the wind and the rain,
'Gainst knaves and thieves men shut their gate,
For the rain it raineth every day.

But when I came, alas! to wive,
With hey, ho, the wind and the rain,

By swaggering could I never thrive,
For the rain it raineth every day.

But when I came unto my beds,
With hey, ho, the wind and the rain,
With toss-pots still had drunken heads,
For the rain it raineth every day.

A great while ago the world begun,
With hey, ho, the wind and the rain,
But that's all one, our play is done,
And we'll strive to please you every day.

This song has caused such an amount of conflicting comment, so opposite in its conclusions, that I append a few excerpts to assist the reader in his consideration of its intention and significance.

George P. Goodale, the dramatic critic, incorporates the view of Charles Knight in one of a series of essays on the subject, published recently, under the caption of "The Kaleidoscope" in *The Detroit Free Press*. He says: "The song of the Clown, originally given as an epilogue, though not retained in the acting editions of the hour, is judiciously regarded as the most philosophical Clown song on record, on the discoverable wis-

dom of which a treatise might be written.
Charles Knight, indeed, goes so far as to charac-
terize it as the history of a life, from the condition
of a little tiny boy, through man's estate, to decaying age. The conclusion is that what is true
of the individual is true of the species, and that
what was of yesterday was also of generations
long passed away—for 'a great while ago the
world begun.' "

Howard Staunton takes another view of the
song, and quotes Stevens, in support of his theory,
in his notes on the subject: "It is to be regretted,
perhaps, that this 'nonsensical ditty,' as Stevens
terms it, has not been long since degraded to the
foot-notes. It was evidently one of those jigs,
with which it was the rude custom of the Clown
to gratify the groundlings upon the conclusion of
a play. These absurd compositions, intended
only as a vehicle for buffoonery, were usually im-
provizations of the singer, tagged to some popular
ballad-burden—or the first lines of various songs
strung together in ludicrous juxtaposition, at the
end of each of which, the performer indulged in

hideous grimace, and a grotesque sort of 'Jump Jim Crow' dance."

Weiss takes a more sentimental view of the song, and, in a somewhat lengthy essay, attaches to it a deep significance, concluding with a tender reference to the Fool in King Lear, who uses some of the lines of the same song, but with a far different motive. ["When the play is over, . . . Feste is left alone upon the stage. Then he sings a song which conveys to us his feeling of the world's partiality: all things proceed according to law; nobody is humored; people must abide the consequence of their actions, 'for the rain it raineth every day.' A 'little tiny boy' may have his toy; but a man must guard against knavery and thieving: marriage itself cannot be sweetened by swaggering; whoso drinks with 'toss-pots' will get a 'drunken head': it is a very old world, and began so long ago that no change in its habits can be looked for. The grave insinuation of this song is touched with the vague, soft bloom of the play. . . . The note is hardly more presageful than the cricket's stir in the late silence of a summer. How gracious hath Shakespeare been to mankind in this play. He could not do otherwise than leave Feste all alone to pronounce its benediction, for his heart was a nest of songs whence they rose to whistle with the air of wisdom. Alas for the poor fool in Lear who sang to drown the cries from a violated nest."

I wish that I could take the same view as Dr. Weiss of the song and the singer. It is not only ingenious but poetical in the extreme and is a reflex of the gentle nature and sweet fancy of the writer; but with exception of the love songs, sung as a minstrel, I do not find a line of poetry in the part of the jester, nor a single expression of sincere or even simulated sentimentality.

Lloyd seems to have summed up the character concisely when he says: "He knows the world too well . . . to feel much sympathy for anybody, or consequently to get much in return." While Ulrici goes still further and asserts: "He (Feste) alone in full consciousness contemplates life as a merry Twelfth Night,—in-which-every one has, in fact, only to play his allotted part to the greatest possible amusement of himself and others."

For my part I think the song is the conventional conclusion of the play, appropriate, but with no special significance.

The same design is followed in "Love's Labor's Lost," and the "Midsummer Night's Dream"; they both terminate with a song.   Epilogues conclude "As You Like It" and "Henry VIII"; and Chorus closes the historical plays.   The tragedies alone close with the culminating incident.

I recall when almost every form of dramatic composition closed with a "Tag," and it was one of the superstitions of the dramatic profession, that to speak the tag at rehearsal augured failure.

LAUNCELOT GOBBO

IN

THE MERCHANT OF VENICE

"*A Merry Devil*"

IN that delightful comedy, "The Merchant of Venice," we have a type of the shrewd but ignorant serving man, or boy, drawn on the same lines as Launce and Speed in "The Two Gentlemen of Verona," and the two Dromios, in "The Comedy of Errors," but apparently younger and less matured than either of them.

His name is Launcelot Gobbo, a fact of which he is somewhat proud. He has a crude philosophy and a rude kind of wit. He uses big words and misapplies them most ingenuously. He is good-natured, full of fun, and rejoices in a practical jest.

Launcelot is the servant to Shylock, a wealthy Jewish merchant and money lender of Venice, with whom he lives and of whom he stands in wholesome awe. His fun-loving nature, however, has served to brighten the dull and dreary home of that stern and revengeful gentleman, a fact that Jessica, the Jew's daughter, frankly acknowledges in her first interview with the boy.

> Our house is hell, and thou a merry devil
> Did'st rob it of some taste of tediousness.

Launcelot does not appear till the second scene of the second act of the comedy, when we find him stealthily leaving his master's house. We learn that he feels aggrieved at some apparent wrong at the hands of his employer, and is debating whether to remain in his service, or to run away. His soliloquy or self-argument on the point is most entertaining. He would be just, but being both plaintiff and defendant, as well as advocate and judge of the question at issue, he can scarcely be credited with impartiality. However, the motives that he frankly acknowledges, and the reasons he advances are most delightfully human, and most humorously expressed. The entire passage is a quaint, and by no means unnatural, self-contention between duty and inclination; the conclusion, as a matter of course, being in favor of inclination.

Certainly, my conscience will serve me to run from this Jew, my master: the fiend is at mine elbow, and tempts me, saying to me, "Gobbo, Launcelot Gobbo, good Launcelot, or good Gobbo, or good Launcelot Gobbo, use your legs, take the start, run away." My conscience says—"No; take heed, honest Launcelot; take heed, honest Gobbo; or," as aforesaid, "honest Launcelot Gobbo; do not run; scorn running with thy heels."—Well, the most courageous fiend bids me pack; *via!* says the fiend; away, says the fiend; for the heavens rouse up a brave mind, says the fiend, and run. Well, my conscience, hanging about the neck of my heart, says very wisely to me—"my honest friend Launcelot, being an honest man's son"—or rather an honest woman's son;—for, indeed, my father did something smack, something grow to,—he had a kind of taste;—well, my conscience says—'Launcelot, budge not;" "budge," says the fiend; 'budge not," says my conscience. Conscience, say I, you counsel well; fiend, say I, you counsel well; to be ruled by my conscience, I should stay with the Jew, my master, who, Heaven bless the mark! is a kind of devil; and, to run away from the Jew, I should be ruled by the fiend, who, saving your reverence, is the devil himself: certainly, the Jew is the very devil incarnation, and, in my conscience, my conscience is but a kind of hard conscience, to offer to counsel me to stay with the Jew: the fiend gives the more friendly counsel! I will run; fiend, my heels are at your commandment, I will run.

However, Launcelot does not run; he is spared that violence to his conscientious scruples by the unexpected advent of his father, an old Italian peasant, whose voice is heard calling in the distance, and halts the would-be runaway.

Launcelot's decision of character is not very marked, nor his resentments very strong, for in a moment his wrongs are forgotten, and he is designing a practical jest on his aged parent.

"O heavens!" he exclaims, "this is my true-begotten father; who, being more than sand-blind, high-gravel-blind, knows me not:—I will try confusions with him."

Old Gobbo, bent with age, almost blind, and feeling his way by the aid of a staff, hobbles on the scene; he carries a small basket on his arm, and in a voice of "childish treble" cries: "Master young gentleman, I pray you, which is the way to master Jew's?"

Launcelot takes the old fellow by the shoulders, and turns him first to the right, then to the left, and finally completely round, giving him the following, somewhat confusing directions: "Turn up on your right hand at the next turning, but at the next turning of all, on your left; marry, at the very next turning, turn of no hand, but turn down directly to the Jew's house."

Small wonder that the old man exclaims: "By God's sonties, 'twill be a hard way to hit."

However, he is seeking and most anxious to find his son, and as soon as he has recovered from the jolting he has received at the hands of his demonstrative informant, he asks him the following most extraordinary and confusing question: "Can you tell me whether one Launcelot, that dwells with him, dwell with him, or no?"

This is excellent matter for the boy to try confusions with, so he answers question with question, prefacing it, however, with an aside, "Mark me now; now will I raise the waters. Talk you of young Master Launcelot?"

But the old man will not admit that his son

is entitled to the dignity of "Master" Launcelot:
so that eccentric young gentleman, who certainly
has a novel sense of humor, tells him that his son
is dead. The sincere grief of the old man evidently shames the boy, for he quickly changes
his tone, and asks: "Do you know me, father?"

Old Gobbo pitifully replies: "Alack, sir, I
am sand blind; I know you not."

This induces some shrewd observations from
Launcelot, which are worthy of note: "If you
had your eyes, you might fail of the knowing me:
it is a wise father that knows his own child."

Launcelot then kneels down with his back to
his father, and continues: "Give me your blessing: truth will come to light, murder cannot be
hid long, a man's son may, but in the end truth
will out."

The old man has been deceived once and hesitates; upon which Launcelot exclaims with some
impatience: "Pray you, let's have no more fooling about it, but give me your blessing; I am
Launcelot, your boy that was, your son that is,
your child that shall be."

Still the old man is not convinced, and protests: "I cannot think you are my son."

To which Launcelot answers: "I know not what I shall think of that; but I am sure Margery, your wife, is my mother."

This is conclusive, and Old Gobbo proceeds to lay his hand upon his son's head to give him his blessing; but Launcelot having knelt with his back towards him, the paternal hand encounters the back of the boy's head which is crowned with a luxurious growth of hair, and causes the old man to exclaim: "Lord worshipp'd might he be! what a beard thou hast got: thou hast got more hair on thy chin than Dobbin, my fill-horse, has on his tail."

Which informs us, that though "exceeding poor," Gobbo is sufficiently well off to own a shaft horse, and as he subsequently states, he has brought a dish of doves as a present to Launcelot's master, we may infer that he and his wife Margery cultivate a piece of ground, or a small farm outside the city; and possibly raise pigeons and doves, a not uncommon industry among the

Italian peasantry. Having established his identity with his father, Launcelot proceeds to tell him of his intention to run away from the Jew's service, and we gather his reason to be, that he does not get sufficient food to satisfy his youthful appetite; but perhaps the fact that the Lord Bassanio is engaging servants, and giving them "rare new liveries," may be the temptation.

The contemptuous reference to the Jewish race by this ignorant boy, and his vulgar pun on the word Jew are significant indications of the general prejudice against the Jews at this period; not only in Venice, but in all parts of the civilized world.

Well, well; but, for mine own part, as I have set up my rest to run away, so I will not rest till I have run some ground. My master's a very Jew; give him a present! give him a halter; I am famish in his service; you may tell every finger I have with my ribs. Father, I am glad you are come; give me your present to one Master Bassanio, who indeed gives rare new liveries; if I serve not him, I will run as far as God has any ground.—O rare fortune! here comes the man:—to him, father; for I am a Jew if I serve the Jew any longer.

The interview between Old Gobbo, his son, and the Lord Bassanio is delightfully entertaining. Launcelot's usual volubility halts in the presence of the young nobleman, and his father's assistance becomes necessary to prefer the suit "impertinent" to himself, and express "the very defect of the matter." However, the suit is granted, and Launcelot is instructed to take leave of his old master, and report at the lodgings of his new employer. The self-satisfaction of Master Launcelot at his success is most humorously expressed, and with an egotism equally amusing; while his optimistic views of the future, obtained from the lines in his hand, indicate a confidence in the science of palmistry, which the author evidently does not share.

Father, in.—I cannot get a service, no; I have ne'er a tongue in my head.—Well, if any man in Italy have a fairer table, which doth offer to swear upon a book! —I shall have good fortune.—Go to, here's a simple line of life; here's a small trifle of wives; alas! fifteen wives is nothing! eleven widows and nine maids is a simple coming-in for one man; and then to 'scape drowning thrice, and to be in peril of my life from

the edge of a feather bed,—here are simple 'scapes.
Well, if Fortune be a woman, she's a good wench
for this gear.—Father, come; I'll take my leave of
the Jew in the twinkling of an eye.

Notwithstanding his scruples of conscience that
caused him so much anxiety, when we first met
him, Launcelot has not been entirely loyal to his
master, and on leaving we find him secretly bearing a letter from Jessica, the Jew's daughter, to
her young Christian lover, Lorenzo.   The missive requires a reply which Launcelot obtains ver-
bally, and the cunning young rascal cleverly man-
ages to convey it to the young Jewess, while bearing an invitation to her father, from his new master, Bassanio.   His words are not brilliant, but
serve to indicate his ingenuity.

> Mistress, look out at window, for all this;
> There will come a Christian by,
> Will be worth a Jewess' eye.

Launcelot accompanies his new master to Bel-
mont, where on our next meeting we find him
comfortably installed; very much at home, and
in a new livery.   He is still bandying words with

Jessica, who is now the wife of Lorenzo, and, in the absence of Portia, mistress of the house. His self-esteem seems to have grown in his new service, his vocabulary has increased, and he speaks with more authority, but with the same unfortunate propensity for punning. He is obviously favored by his "betters," and like many others of small mind takes advantage of that fact to speak with a freedom that is not entirely devoid of impudence. However, his humor atones for much, and his good-nature accomplishes the rest.

The dialogue quoted (with some slight eliminations) below takes place in the garden of Portia's house (Act 3, Scene 5). It is apparently the continuation of a discussion of the old theme of Jessica's parentage, and her father's sins; Launcelot taking a literal view of the scriptural precept in her case.

Laun. Yes, truly; for, look you, the sins of the father are to be laid upon the children; therefore, I promise you, I fear you. I was always plain with you, and so now I speak my agitation of the matter; therefore, be of good cheer; for, truly, I think thou art damned. There is but one hope in it that can do you any good.

Jess. And what hope is that, I pray thee?

Laun. Marry, you may partly hope that you are not the Jew's daughter.

Jess. So the sins of my mother should be visited on me.

Laun. Truly then I fear you are damned both by father and mother; thus when I shun Scylla, your father, I fall into Charybdis, your mother; well, you are gone both ways.

Jess. I shall be saved by my husband; he hath made me a Christian.

Laun. Truly, the more to blame he; we were Christians enow before; e'en as many as could well live, one by another. This making of Christians will raise the price of hogs; if we grow all to be pork-eaters, we shall not shortly have a rasher on the coals for money.

The entrance of Lorenzo puts an end to Launcelot's calamitous predictions, and that gentleman having little appreciation of the latter's verbal fooling, directs him. "Go in, sirrah: bid them prepare for dinner."

To which the irrepressible Launcelot replies: "That is done, sir; they have all stomachs."

With some impatience, Lorenzo exclaims:

"Goodly Lord, what a wit-snapper art thou! then bid them prepare dinner."

This does not discourage the boy, who responds: "That is done too, sir; only, cover is the word."

Lorenzo, with some irritation, seeks to bring this equivocation to a close, and now gives his directions with emphasis: "I pray thee, understand a plain man in his plain meaning; go to thy fellows, bid them cover the table, serve in the meat, and we will come in to dinner."

The imperturbable self-esteem and good-nature of Launcelot is proof, however, against censure or sarcasm; and with unruffled gravity he replies with humorous iteration: "For the table, sir, it shall be served in; for the meat, sir, it shall be covered; for your coming in to dinner, sir, why, let it be as humors and conceits shall govern."

And having thus delivered himself, Launcelot makes a dignified exit from the scene.

Lorenzo's apostrophe to Launcelot's discourse is an admirable summary of the shallow mind, that mistakes the mere jugglery of words for wit.

It was a favorite method of Shakespeare's to
furnish humor in his "simples" and serving men,
and proved an amusing diversion in their mouths:
but, in others, it is the unconscious tribute that
ignorance and incapacity pays to knowledge and
distinction.

> *Lor.*   O dear discretion, how his words are suited!
> The fool hath planted in his memory
> An army of good words; and I do know
> A many fools that stand in better place,
> Garnish'd like him, that for a tricksy word
> Defy the matter.

Launcelot makes one more brief appearance, to
announce the early return of Bassanio to Bel-
mont, and as a harbinger of glad tidings we leave
him in the service of a noble master and a gracious mistress.

The business of the Shakespearean clowns is
traditional.   It has been handed down by comedians from generation to generation.   It was
familiar to every stage manager of experience, in
the days of the resident stock company; and any
departure from the conventional business of these

Charles Charters as "Launcelot Gobbo" in "The Merchant
of Venice"

parts was, until recently, viewed with disapproval, and regarded as presumption.

A most interesting and unique performance of Launcelot Gobbo was given some years ago by that sterling character actor, Mr. Robert Peyton Carter, so long associated with Miss Maude Adams. I was the Shylock of the performance to which I refer. Mr. Carter's Launcelot was not a boy, but a humorous and mischievous young man. At no time during the performance, even when trembling with fear before his master, was a smile absent from his face; with this result, the audience were smiling all the time Launcelot was in view. You knew, as you looked at him during his self-argument between duty and inclination, that his mind was already made up to run away, and that his conscientious scruples (if he really ever had any) were overcome before he uttered them. His practical jest with his father, when he misdirects him to the Jew's house, indicated that it was but a sample of the pranks the young man had played upon him all his life, and the bright twinkle in his eyes as his young mistress called him "a merry devil" connoted a thousand tricks that the young rascal had played during the term of his service in the Jew's house and robbed that somewhat dreary residence of its "taste of tediousness."

Mr. Carter's business on the delivery of Jessica's letter to Lorenzo was original and good; his exaggerated obeisance to the several friends in company with that gentleman being particularly characteristic and happy.   In the last act of the comedy, too frequently omitted in representation, Mr. Carter's appreciation of Shakespearean humor was manifest.   The importance of his new employment, his vanity in his "rare new livery," and confidence of privileged service were delightfully presented, and rounded out a performance as notable as it was consistent and effective.

"The Merchant of Venice" held an important place in the repertoire of the late Mr. Richard Mansfield.   In discussing the various characters in the play with that distinguished gentleman, he told me he considered the Launcelot Gobbo of Mr. A. G. Andrews, of his company, the best he had ever seen. It did not surprise me, for I knew Mr. Andrews to be a thorough and painstaking artist, studying out to the most minute detail every point of his make-up, costume and business. Mr. Andrews presented Launcelot as a boy to whom life was a very serious problem. His costume was extremely characteristic; his doublet and trunks were worn and patched, his hose seamed and darned, and his sandal-shoes with their leather straps had seen service hard and long. He made his first entrance from his master's house hastily, then looked round fearfully and, finding himself unobserved, sat down upon the door-step and seriously held self-communion as to the justice of leaving his master's service. In other respects he followed the traditional business of the part; but nothing was exaggerated, rather subdued; his object being to present Launcelot as a possible human being, and not an impossible clown, as many comedians have done. The humor of the part was always present, never intruded, but conveyed naturally and without effort: the result being a well proportioned and artistic performance.

CITIZEN

IN

JULIUS CÆSAR

THE tragedy of "Julius Cæsar" is so exalted in theme, so heroic in sentiment and so noble in principle, that humor would scarcely be an appropriate factor in its composition. The magnitude of manhood that the author has brought into such striking contrast and juxtaposition is so completely sustained, and the elements of lofty patriotism and civic virtue are preserved so exclusively, that the lesser qualities and conditions of life are dwarfed into insignificance.

The characters of Marcus Brutus, Cassius, Marc Antony, Cæsar, Casca, Trebonius and the others, are cast in such "heroic mold," that they represent "the highest heaven of invention," and like Chorus, in the prologue to "Henry V," we might well ask:

A kingdom for a stage, princes to act
And monarchs to behold the swelling scene!

However, before the great personages in the
drama make their appearance, Shakespeare has
given us an illustration of the character of the
Roman populace, and has introduced an episode
that serves as a foundation for the later incidents,
and at the same time furnishes an excellent example of broad comedy and wholesome humor.

It is in the first scene of the play, which is
simply described as "Rome.   A Street."   A number of citizens are assembled; a typical crowd of
mechanics, artisans, serving-men, and idlers, who
are awaiting the advent of the procession to the
ceremonies of the feast of the Lupercal.   They
are - good-naturedly but somewhat boisterously
jostling, and shouting, when they are interrupted
by the approach of two of the tribunes, Flavius
and Marullus, who in turn silence, reprove and
question them.

The dialogue between the characters briefly informs us of the sumptuary laws of Rome at that
period, and indicates the sentiments and relations

that existed between the patricians and the common people.

In the assemblage, two only of the citizens reply to the questions of the tribunes; they have no names in the list of characters, but are simply distinguished as "First" and "Second" citizens.

The first citizen is an ordinary mechanic, distinguished by no especial feature from the rest of the crowd; but the wit and humor of the second warrants some description.

In many places that I have visited, I have found a local wit or jester. The community is usually very proud of him, and he is brought forward on all social occasions to sustain the reputation of the town for humor, and its appreciation. These alleged wits vary in condition, but never in characteristic. They are usually fat, ruddy-faced and good-natured, with a stock of well-seasoned wit and fully matured stories which they exploit and relate much to their own satisfaction and the admiration of their local admirers, but not always to the enjoyment of the visitor. Whatever they say is supposed to be witty, and they are at all times ready for a verbal passage at arms with any one who has the temerity to challenge them. This type is not rare, but occasionally one meets a natural wit who is both mellow and keen. Such an one I imagine the individual to be who appears under the title of the "Second Citizen" in "Julius Cæsar."

The man is a cobbler by trade, and a wit by nature; his replies to the questions of the tribunes are respectful, but each of them is accompanied by a jest which in the presentation of the play is followed by a hearty laugh from his fellows, to indicate their appreciation, and his popularity with them.

The scene, as I before observed, is brief and largely self-explanatory; I therefore give the text in full without further comment:

Flavius.   Hence! home, you idle creatures, get you
                home.
            Is this a holiday? What! know you not,
            Being mechanical, you ought not walk,
            Upon a laboring day, without the sign
            Of your profession? Speak, what trade
                art thou?

First Cit. Why, sir, a carpenter.

Marullus. Where is thy leather apron, and thy rule?

What dost thou with thy best apparel on?

You, sir, what trade are you?

Second Cit. Truly, sir, in respect of a fine workman, I am but, as you would say, a cobbler.

Marullus. But what trade art thou? Answer me directly.

Second Cit. A trade, sir, that, I hope, I may use with a safe conscience; which is indeed, sir, a mender of bad soles.

Marullus. What trade, thou knave? thou naughty knave, what trade?

Second Cit. Nay, I beseech you, sir, be not out with me: yet, if you be out, sir, I can mend you.

Marullus. What mean'st thou by that? Mend me, thou saucy fellow?

Second Cit. Why, sir, cobble you.

Flavius. Thou art a cobbler, art thou?

Second Cit. Truly, sir, all that I live by is with the awl: I meddle with no tradesman's matters, nor women's matters but with awl. I am indeed, sir, a surgeon to old shoes; when they are in great danger, I re-cover them. As proper men as ever trod upon neats-leather have gone upon my handiwork.

Flavius. But wherefore art not in thy shop to-day?

Why dost thou lead these men about the streets?

Second Cit. Truly, sir, to wear out their shoes, to get myself into more work. But indeed, sir, we make holiday to see Cæsar and to rejoice in his triumph.

The cobbler's reply brings even a more severe reproof from the tribunes, but trumpets are heard in the distance, the procession is seen approaching, and the censures of the patricians are unheeded as the citizens disperse in the direction of the coming spectacle.

An amusing incident occurred in a notable performance of "Julius Cæsar" given some years ago in San Francisco.

As a matter of interest I mention the cast of the principal characters, all of the actors having since passed away.

Brutus............Mr. Edwin Booth
Cassius.............Mr. Barton Hill
Marc Antony...Mr. John McCullough
Julius Cæsar.....Mr. Henry Edwards

All of these characters, with others, enter on the first scene in a procession returning from the games of the Lupercal, and are followed by a crowd of citizens. Cæsar, impressed by an act of marked discourtesy on the part of the lean and hungry Cassius, calls Marc Antony to his side, and exclaims: "Let me have men about me that are fat." Upon this, the two comedians playing the First and Second Citizens, Mr. C. B. Bishop and Mr. William Mestayer, both of very robust figures, and each turning the scales at 250 pounds at least, advanced, one on either side of Cæsar, and placing their hands on their rotund and protruding stomachs, looked up at the great man as much as to say, "Well! here is just what you want."

Of course, this interpolation of business caused considerable amusement both for the audience and the actors, and completely destroyed the dignity of the scene; but both gentlemen were great personal favorites with the public, and their little joke was tolerated by their indulgent friends as in evidence of their eccentricity, in spite of its absurd and inappropriate introduction.

The two comedians have long since joined "the great majority," their exuberant humor is but a memory, but it is still affectionately cherished in the sphere in which they lived.

The citizens appear on several occasions during the progress of the tragedy, notably, in the Senate scene at the assassination of Cæsar, and later, in the market-place, where they are addressed in turn by Brutus and Marc Antony. Their lines are merely acquiescent to the sentiments of the principal characters; but there is one line that always struck me as humorous in the extreme. It occurs in Act 3, Scene 2, after the first part of Marc Antony's address over the body of Cæsar. Antony, apparently overcome by emotion, pauses in his eloquent argument in defense of his dead friend, when the First Citizen sagely remarks: "Methinks there is much reason in his sayings." To which our old friend, the Second Citizen replies: "If thou consider rightly of the matter, Cæsar hath had great wrong."

It is to this last speech that I refer. His absurdly inadequate expression of sympathy for the great man who has been so foully murdered, and whose body lies before him covered with wounds, always seemed to me to carry with it a sense of the ridiculous, that I could never completely overcome; although I am prepared to admit that, per se, it is not inappropriate to the limited intelligence of the speaker.

There is a brief episode in the next scene of the same act in which the citizens again appear, that has a delightful touch of satirical humor.   It occurs after the people have been aroused to vengeance against the conspirators by the address of Marc Antony, and are seeking the assassins in the streets of the city.   Among many suspicious persons accosted by the crowd is Cinna, the poet, who is seized and assailed by a perfect volley of questions from the excited multitude; to which he replies: "What is my name?   Whither am I going?   Where do I dwell?   Am I a married man or a bachelor?   Then to answer every man directly, and briefly, wisely, and truly; wisely I say, I am a bachelor."

To this our ever-humorous friend the Second Citizen, who is one of the foremost in the crowd, and evidently a married man, responds in characteristic fashion: "That's as much as to say, they are fools that marry; you'll bear me a bang for that, I fear."

Further questioning reveals the name of the captured man to be Cinna, which being also the name of one of the conspirators, for whom he is mistaken, the crowd cry: "Tear him to pieces, he is a conspirator!"

The poor fellow, however, protests: "I am Cinna, the poet; I am Cinna, the poet."

Cinna's poetry does not appear to be highly appreciated by the people, or he has unfortunately encountered an unsympathetic critic, for one of the citizens exclaims: "Tear him for his bad verses; tear him for his bad verses."

Again the poet protests: "I am not Cinna, the conspirator."

Whatever justice there may have been in the fate adjudged the poor poet by the enraged populace, our ingenuous friend, the Second Citizen, is not without mercy, and he proposes: "It is no matter; his name's Cinna; pluck but his name out of his heart, and turn him going."

Which suggests the significance of the trite old adage, "Save us from our friends."

In a memorable production of "Julius Cæsar," at Booth's Theater, New York, in the early seventes, a most excellent actor, Mr. Charles Leclerq, played the Second Citizen, and gave it an importance and significance I had never before witnessed. Mr. Leclerq was tall and of spare figure; and his natural manner incisive rather than unctuous. His conceptions were the result of well-digested thought, and his performances rounded and compete. Surrounded by his homely fellows, and confident of their support, he was important but not intrusive, and impressed his audience with the characteristics I have endeavored to describe, so that, when one left the theater, in spite of the overwhelming predominance of the other characters, Mr. Leclerq's performance of the homely old Roman cobbler lingered in the memory.

THE CLOWN
IN
ANTONY AND CLEOPATRA

IN that most excellent work entitled "Studies in Shakespeare," by Richard Grant White, the author gives some sound advice to students and readers of the poet, which I most heartily indorse: "Don't skip small parts, such as servants, clowns, rustics, etc.; read them all."

This suggestion cannot be too emphatically impressed upon the minds of young readers, who, eager for the development of the plot or for the main points of the story, frequently neglect or omit the minor parts, deeming them non-essential to the interest of the play. This is to be deplored; for Shakespeare has placed many of his best thoughts and most pointed epigrams in the mouths of comparatively unimportant characters; so that to pass over or neglect these passages is to lose

many beauties of thought, much philosophic re-
lection, and a fund of characteristic humor.

From the rich mine of his transcendent genius,
the poet has drawn such a wealth of wit and wisdom, that he has endowed the peasant as liberally
as the prince, and the clown as the courtier; the
flashes of brilliancy that sparkle in the repartee of
the prince become bits of homely humor in the
simple dialogue of the peasant, and the compliment of the courtier is bluntly expressed in the
rugged honesty of the clown. The garb, becoming and appropriate, is fitted to the wearer; the
coublet to the one, the smock to the other.

In all of his rustic and humorous characters,
Shakespeare has been most conservative of their
possibilities; probably from the fact that prior to
his time, and also during his early career on the
stage, the clown monopolized the attention of the
audience to the exclusion of the serious interest of
the play, and was usually a most exaggerated cari-
cature without sense or significance.

Shakespeare felt this condition keenly and expressed himself emphatically on the subject; espe-

cially in the prince's instructions to the player in Hamlet (Act 3, Scene 2.) He set himself about to reform the evil, by keeping the clown and the comedian within the limits of "the modesty of nature."

The brief sketch of the bucolic clown in "Antony and Cleopatra" is distinctly Shakespearean in character, and it is to be regretted that he does not appear at greater length in the play. While the tragedy is located in Egypt, the clown is essentially English, and is a capital type of the country clodhopper, many of whom still survive in remote English villages to-day, and such as the poet saw daily at Stratford when a boy.

This clown is a stockily-built, ruddy-faced man, with a shock head of hair, dressed in a homespun or coarse canvas smock, awkwardly stamping into the apartment, stolidly indifferent to conditions or environment, bent only on the execution of his commission, which is to bring "the pretty worm of Nilus, that kills and pains not," concealed in a basket of figs to some unknown lady. He is insensible to the significance of his errand, ignorant of its design, but honest in his warning as to the dangerous character of the worm; and what a powerful dramatic contrast is presented by the introduction of this dense, slow-witted fellow as an instrument to bring the means of death to the imperious "Sorceress of the Nile," now a hopeless despairing woman; "Tho' uncrowned, yet still a queen and daughter of a king."

At first he is denied admission by the soldier guards, but he creates such a disturbance, and the contents of his basket appear to be so harmless, that on the queen's intervention, the clown is permitted to enter her presence.

The fellow is ignorant of the exalted rank of his patron, and entirely lacking in reverence, for he pays the queen no deference, but gabbles on insensible of dismissal and oblivious to interruption till his tale is finished.

Cleopatra asks: "Hast thou the pretty worm of Nilus there?" To which he replies: "Truly I have him; but I would not be the party that should desire you to touch him, for his biting is immortal; those that do die of it do seldom or never recover."

The perversion of language in the above is delicious, and to my mind equal to anything that Dogberry says in "Much Ado About Nothing"; and is another example of Shakespeare's favorite method of expressing humor by the misuse of words by his clowns and fools.

Ignoring the warning of the clown, the queen eagerly inquires: "Rememb'rest thou any that have died on't?" To which the garrulous old fellow responds: "Very many, men and women, too. I heard of one of them no longer than yesterday; a very honest woman, but something given to lie, as a woman should not do but in the way of honesty; how she died of the biting of it, what pain she felt. Truly she makes a very good report of the worm; but he that will believe all that they say, shall never be saved by half that they do."

The unconscious but direct reference to Cleopatra herself in the above is passed without notice, or in the extremity of her grief, unperceived; and the clown is dismissed.

But the fellow is not to be gotten rid of so easily; he starts to go, but returns repeatedly with continued warnings as to the dangerous character of the worm: "Look you, the worm is not to be trusted," and "Give it nothing, I pray you, for it is not worth the feeding."

To this last admonition, Cleopatra inquires: "Will it eat me?" The clown takes this question as a reflection on himself, and replies with some emphasis: "You must not think I am so simple, but I know the devil himself will not eat a woman; I know that a woman is a dish for the gods, if the devil dress her not. But, truly, these same whoreson devils do the gods great harm in their women, for in every ten that they make, the devils mar five." And with the parting salutation: "I wish you joy of the worm," the clown finally takes his departure.

Ordinary students of Shakespeare must have noted that in spite of the fact that the poet has given us some of the noblest ideals of womanhood, there are passages in his plays of the keenest satire, and bitterest denunciation of women.

How far his own unfortunate experience with the sex may have influenced his mind, it is not my purpose to discuss here; but in the two passages spoken by the clown, that I have quoted above, I cannot but think there is an echo from the heart of the man, that as the poet sounds the key-note of an uncongenial marriage, an unappreciative mistress, and a friend's duplicity.

It is interesting to note, that in the two great tragedies, "Julius Cæsar" and "Antony and Cleopatra," the only scenes of humor, in both instances equally brief, are placed, in the former at the beginning of the play, and in the latter almost at its conclusion.

THE GRAVE-DIGGERS

IN

HAMLET

"Has this fellow no feeling of his business, that he sings at grave-making?"

IT would scarcely seem possible that a grave-yard attached to a church, with a half-dug grave in the foreground, for the scene; midnight or near thereto, for the time; a pickax, a spade, a heap of fresh earth, some human skulls and bones for the properties; and two grave-diggers for the dramatis personæ would furnish a location and material for comedy and humor, yet in the first scene of the fifth act of the tragedy of "Hamlet," Shakespeare has taken these materials and con-ditions, and given us a series of incidents, a variety of character, and a dialogue replete with the most delightful comedy, brilliant repartee, ready wit and subtle humor.

The circumstances are these: A young lady attached to the court of the King of Denmark has been drowned. The general opinion being that she committed suicide. In the time of Shakespeare, and prior thereto, such unfortunates were denied Christian burial. Their remains were interred outside of consecrated ground without service or any of the rites of the Church. In fact, it was not unusual to bury them at the intersection of the highways, very deeply, and to drive a strong stake through the body. The object of this barbarous proceeding being, to empale and destroy the evil spirit, which the prevailing superstition supposed to be in possession of the suicide. In the present instance, the King has commanded that the remains of the unfortunate lady should be buried in the consecrated ground of the churchyard.

The King's command, violating all the ancient and accepted traditions of the church, arouses the indignation of the old sexton, who combines the office of grave-digger. To this personage Shakespeare has given such a strong individuality, such a pungency of wit and wealth of humor, together with such delightful touches of nature, making it so true to life, that I cannot but think the poet must have had a prototype in his own observation and experience.

In the list of characters in the play this personage and his assistant are set down as "Two Clowns as Grave-diggers," but modern editors have separated them in the cast, and called them "First and Second Grave-diggers." This method has been adopted in all the acting editions, and in the following observations I shall so designate them.

The first grave-digger is of a type that may be found in many of our country villages to-day,—a quaint sententious old fellow "dressed in a little brief authority," and full of his own importance. He has a little knowledge of law, quotes one or two legal phrases in Latin incorrectly, and preaches a crude idea of socialism to his younger assistant, much to the awe and admiration of that simple individual, who addresses his acknowledged superior as "Goodman delver."

I picture the old fellow in my mind as robust of figure, ruddy of feature, with distinct evidences of bibulous taste on his nose and cheeks, a humorous twinkle in his eyes, in spite of an assumed severity, dressed in the homely smock of the peasant of that place and period, and about fifty years of age. He has the courage of his convictions for he has seldom found any one to combat them, so he advances his arguments with the authority of one whose dictum is not to be questioned. Should these fail him, however, he can command the respect of his fellows by a ready tongue and homely wit, as exampled in his dialogue with his subordinate, and later with Prince Hamlet.

He is no respecter of persons: his replies to the questions of Hamlet being as straightforward and blunt as those to his peasant companion, while his replications in the exchange of wit with the former indicate so much irreverence and independence, that it draws from the Prince the significant observation: "By the Lord, Horatio, . . .

the age is grown so picked that the toe of the peasant comes so near the heel of the courtier, he galls his kibe."

The character of the old sexton bears in some small degree a resemblance to that of "Dogberry" in "Much Ado About Nothing," in its self-importance, but it is more consistent, less bombastic, and never servile.

Our first acquaintance with the old fellow is made at the beginning of the first scene of the fifth act of the play, when he enters the church-yard followed by his assistant, who carries a spade and a mattock. That his mind is disturbed by the violation of ancient traditions is evidenced in his first speech given in the form of a question to his follower: "Is she to be buried in Christian burial that willfully seeks her own salvation?" To which his assistant, evidently a younger man, with the assurance of accurate information, re-plies: "I tell thee she is; and therefore make her grave straight: the crowner hath sat on her and finds it Christian burial."

Now comes the inherent love of argument in the old man: "How can that be, unless she drowned herself in her own defense?"

The younger man has no reply to this proposition, but contents himself with reiteration: "Why, 'tis found so." To the ordinary peasant of the time this would have concluded the matter, but the sexton, who has small respect for the verdict of the crowner's quest, and perceiving an opportunity to expound his wisdom, proceeds with his argument.

It requires little imagination to realize the pomposity of the sturdy old stickler for tradition, as he emphasizes his points; or to note the syllabic orotundity with which he utters the Latin phrase that he has probably heard in some legal proceedings, and memorized for use at a future time, to awe his adversary with his learning; and to observe the originality of his logic in the conclusion that the lady's death was not accidental. "It must be 'se offendendo'; it cannot be else. For here lies the point: if I drown myself wittingly, it argues an act: and an act hath three branches;

it is, to act, to do, and to perform: argal, she drowned herself wittingly."

His assistant is not without some self-assertion in spite of Latin and logic, and makes a valiant attempt to enter a protest against the old man's prejudiced conclusions. "Nay, but hear you, goodman delver." But the goodman will not be silenced with flattery nor does he propose to honor his youthful disputant with more controversy, but proceeds to demonstrate his theory in a practical fashion. Taking his spade he lays it down on the smooth turf of the church-yard, explaining: "Here lies the water; good." Then at some little distance from the spade he stands the pick or mattock on end: "Here stands the man, good," and taking a position between the two implements, with judicial gravity, he delivers himself as follows: "If the man go to this water and drown himself, it is will he, nill he, he goes; mark you that; but if the water come to him and drown him, he drowns not himself: argal, he that is not guilty of his own death shortens not his own life."

This demonstration almost convinces the rustic skeptic, but he is still in doubt as to the legal aspect of the case, and inquires: "But is this law?" "Ay, marry, is't; crowner's quest law," concludes the old man.

Finding no argument to combat this conclusion, the young fellow falls back on the elemental socialistic question of human inequality. "Will you ha' the truth on't? If this had not been a gentlewoman, she should have been buried out o' Christian burial." The old fellow fully indorses this proposition, and emphasizes it with a still more forcible example, though, perhaps some may not recognize the advantages of the special privileges quoted. "Why, there thou sayest: and the more pity that great folks should have countenance in this world to drown or hang themselves, more than their even-Christian. Come, my spade." The old man takes his spade, but before proceeding to work, asserts the natural dignity of his trade, and bemoans the degeneracy of the age; which provokes the following bit of delightful equivoque:

1st Gra. There is no ancient gentlemen but gardeners, ditchers and grave-makers: they hold up Adam's profession.

2nd Gra. Was he a gentleman?

1st Gra. A' the first that ever bore arms.

2nd Gra. Why, he had none.

1st Gra. What, art a heathen? How dost thou understand the Scripture? The Scripture says Adam digged: Could he dig without arms?

After a hearty laugh at the jest, the old fellow propounds a conundrum, a very popular form of entertainment among simple country wits. However, to realize the significance of the riddle and the preceding dialogue, it is essential to have the full picture in one's mind: the solemn background of the church, the grim environment of the old headstones and tombs, ghostlike in the midnight shadows, the newly made grave waiting for its tenant, the odor of the fresh earth, and the homely figures of the two sextons with the dismal tools of their trade, form a combination in strong contrast with the humor of the dialogue, and yet in complete harmony with the spirit of the occasion. The old grave-digger standing with one foot on his spade, his eyes sparkling with humor, emphasizes with his index finger the question that is to confuse the wits of his younger assistant; the other leaning on the mattock listens with parted lips, eager to catch every word, and match his wit against that of the veteran humorist.

"What is he that builds stronger than either the mason, the shipwright, or the carpenter?"

The young man is puzzled for a moment, scratches his head, then with a look of triumph, answers quickly: "The gallows-maker; for that frame outlives a thousand tenants."

It is a good answer and the old fellow is not slow to acknowledge it, but it is not the correct one, so the momentary satisfaction of the young man is turned to chagrin, and his wits spurred to another effort. How the old fellow chuckles as the young one wrestles with the knotty problem, and how deliciously is the patronage of the old egotist's superior wisdom expressed in the passage that follows: "I like thy wit well, in good faith: The gallows does well: but how does it well? It does well to those that do ill: now thou dost ill to say the gallows is built stronger than

the church: argal: the gallows may do well to thee.
To't again, come."

The young man repeats the proposition: "Who
builds stronger than a mason, a shipwright, or a
carpenter?" and ruefully struggles to find another
fitting reply. But his mental faculties are dull,
it is beyond him, he has to confess it, and the old
fellow does not spare him, but accentuates his
triumph, and completes the poor fellow's humiliation by giving the answer, and then dismissing
him to fetch a stoop of liquor.

"Cudgel thy brains no more about it, for your
dull ass will not mend his pace with beating, and
when you are asked this question next, say 'a
grave-maker': the houses that he makes last till
doomsday. Go, get thee to Yaughan, fetch me a
stoop of liquor."

The traditional business at this point was for
the old grave-digger to remove with great deliberation a number of vests or waist-coats of various
colors and patterns, carefully fold and lay them
at one side, and then roll up his sleeves before
descending into the uncompleted grave to proceed

with his work. This absurd piece of business has, however, long since been discarded, and the actor of to-day plays the part with more appropriate action, consistent with the character, and within scope of human possibility. Laying his spade and pick by the side of the grave he gradually lowers himself into it with the natural effort of a man of his age, then in a workman-like manner proceeds first to loosen the earth with his pick, then to throw it out, together with the skulls and bones as the dialogue calls for them, chanting the words of the old ballad at the proper cues, emphasizing the effort, and punctuating his singing with the strokes of his mattock, and the work of the spade.

It is at this point that Prince Hamlet and his friend Horatio appear outside of the low wall that encloses the grave-yard. Seeing the old man's grim occupation, and hearing his humorous song, the incongruity of the proceeding surprises the Prince, who inquires of his friend: "Has this fellow no feeling of his business that he sings at grave-making?" To which Horatio sagely re-

Louis James as "Pepe" in "Francesco da Rimini"

plies: "Custom hath made it in him a property of easiness."

Unconscious of observation, the sexton continues his work and his song, throwing out the earth, some human bones, and two chapless skulls; while the Prince and his friend look on and philosophize on the gruesome relics that are so irreverently handled by the old man. The second skull thrown from the grave is about to roll away, when the sexton strikes it sharply with his spade to imbed it in the soft, fresh earth. This apparent brutal indifference to the grim remains of poor mortality is the subject of further speculative philosophy on the part of the Prince, who finally steps over the wall, advances to the side of the grave, and addresses the grave-digger, asking: "Who's grave's this, sirrah?"

I imagine the old man has been asked this question so frequently, and by all manner of people, that he has grown impatient at the query, and with scarcely a glance at his questioner he answers abruptly, "Mine, sir," and continues his work and his song.

I recall when I was a very small boy, living in an English country village, an old cobbler,
whose shop, or rather stall, was on the side of the
street by which I went to school. He was a
quaint, good-natured old fellow, and I would frequently stop, watch him at work and talk to him.
All of his work was done by hand. He used
to sit at the end of a low bench on which
were all of his materials and tools, in little
square compartments. He wore a large pair of
spectacles with horn frames, and would bend
over a wooden last, held fast to his knee by a
circular leathern strap from his foot, make holes
with an awl, insert and draw the wax end tightly,
as he attached the upper to the sole of the shoe
he was making. I used to regard him with great
interest, and wonder at his dexterity and rapidity.
I knew practically everybody in the village, and
with boyish curiosity would ask the old cobbler
who the shoes were for. He would invariably
reply: "Mr. Wearem." This puzzled me for
some time, as I knew no one of that name; but
ultimately I comprehended: it was a reproof to

my curiosity, the old man's standing jest, and a whimsical evasion of the question he was asked so frequently. I find a parallel in my old cobbler's jest and the grave-digger's reply to Hamlet.

The Prince, however, is not disposed to be silenced by this discourtesy, but makes a rejoinder that bluntly charges the old man with a ·lie. Against this accusation the grave-digger stoutly defends himself, and makes countercharge with a shrewd wit in a dialogue replete with ingenious punning, and a crude logic that carries his point, and compels recognition from the Prince, who diplomatically changes the subject.

To facilitate the reader's appreciation, I quote the dialogue that follows the grave-digger's reply:

Ham. I think it be thine indeed, for thou liest in't.

Gra. You lie out on't, sir, and therefore 'tis not yours: for my part, I do not lie in't and yet, it is mine.

Ham. Thou dost lie in't, to be in't and to say it is thine: 'tis for the dead, not for the quick: therefore thou liest.

Gra. 'Tis a quick lie, sir, 'twill away again from me to you.

Ham. What man dost thou dig it for?
Gra. For no man, sir.
Ham. What woman then?
Gra. For none neither.
Ham. Who is to be buried in't?
Gra. One that was a woman sir, but, rest her soul, she's dead.

. . . .

Ham. How long hast thou been a grave-maker?

The answer is given with characteristic loquacity, by the old man, who still maintains his reputation as a wit-snapper.

The most casual reader of Shakespeare cannot but observe how much is connoted as well as expressed in many of the brief passages of the poet. In answer to the above simple question, the valor of the late King, and the martial character of the Danes is suggested; we are told the day of Hamlet's birth; we learn of the gossip of the people and the general impression of the Prince's mental condition, the supposed reason of his despatch to England, together with some satirical allusions to the people of that country; and, while the old man ingeniously reveals the age of

Hamlet, he incidentally suggests his own. "I have been sexton here, man and boy, thirty years."

This, granting he was about twenty years old when he began his work as a grave-maker, and it is improbable to suppose that he would be entrusted with such serious work at an earlier age, would make him fifty at this time, as I have before suggested.

Hamlet's next question: "How long will a man lie in the earth ere he rot?" provokes more punning by the old man and some very plain and original reasoning as to the time and process of the decay of mortal remains; those of a tanner in particular.

The dialogue is terminated by the selection of one of the skulls by the grave-digger to illustrate his arguments, which the old man asserts is the skull of Yorick, the late King's jester.

The "property of easiness," suggested by Horatio, is again exampled by the irreverence and familiarity with which the grave-maker handles his skull. As he recalls the pranks of the dead jester, he laughingly slaps the hollow temples of the unconscious remnant, as if he were boxing the ears of the living jester, and gleefully chuckles as memory revives the "mad rogue's" wit and humor, before handing it to the Prince.

This incident diverts the mind of Hamlet from his catechism of the grave-digger to tender memories of his childhood's friend and playmate, so that the sentiment of the scene is changed, but to this I have referred at some length in a former chapter.

The funeral procession enters the church-yard, the sexton assists in lowering the body of the unfortunate lady to its last resting place, and with that duty done, the character of the grave-digger in the play is concluded. But if we permit our imagination a little scope, we might see, after the funeral party has left the scene, the old fellow shoveling the earth back into the newly-tenanted grave, and hear the refrain of his quaint song borne upon the stillness of the early morning air:

> A pick-axe, and a spade, a spade,
> For and a shrouding sheet:

O a pit of clay for to be made
For such a guest is meet.

The most conspicuous figure that I can recall
as a representative of the first grave-digger, was
the late J. H. McVicker, founder and proprietor
of McVicker's Theater, Chicago. He played the
part when en tour with Edwin Booth, his son-in-
law, who was then under his management. I
had the honor of being Mr. Booth's principal support, and played the part of Laertes. Mr. Mc-
Vicker was of Irish and Scotch descent, and combined the general characteristics of those two na-
tionalities. He was strong in his own opinions,
somewhat harsh and dictatorial in his manner,
but with a vein of quaint humor that was much
in evidence when not obsessed with business.
Hardly the temperament for an artist, you would
say? True! but in the case of the old sexton
these very qualities fitted the character. Mr. Mc-
Vicker used little if any make-up, in fact he did
not need any; he was at this time, I should judge,
about sixty years of age, rotund of figure, full in
the face, which was clean-shaven, and with sparse

gray hair, that was always disheveled. He dressed the part in a dark brown tunic or smock; his arms were bare, but his legs and feet were encased in rough buskins and sandals. He looked the part to perfection; he did not have to act, only to speak the lines, and he was the old grave-digger. The self-importance, the grave assumption of knowledge, and the air of "brief authority" over his fellow-worker were finely given; while his surprised expression at the audacity of the younger man in questioning his judgment was a splendid illustration of the assurance of ignorance and self-conceit.

At the time of which I speak (1876) very little, if any, scenery and few properties were carried by touring dramatic companies. We carried none, but depended on the stock of the theaters we visited for the scenery, and borrowed the properties and furniture from local stores, giving in return complimentary tickets to the performance. The two human skulls were especially difficult to obtain in the smaller towns.

Our property-man, however, was of considerable experience and full of resource in an emergency and when unable to obtain the real article invariably found a substitute that served the purpose. For the skulls he used two large turnips, shaping them like the human head, excavating the eye sockets, hollowing the jaws and mouth, and then coloring them with brown paint. Indeed, they looked remarkably well and few of the audience could detect the imposition from the front of the theater. One night, however, when Mr. McVicker, as the grave-digger, handed the supposed skull to Mr. Booth, as Hamlet, the latter gentleman failed to grasp it securely and it fell with a heavy thud to the stage. The deception was then obvious, and the audience roared with laughter. But worse consequences followed. The confounded turnip rolled down to the footlights, knocked off one of the tips of the gas jets (electricity was not then in use), a big flame rose from the broken jet, a cry of Fire! was raised, and a panic in the audience was only averted by the prompt action of the leader of the orchestra, who reached over and smothered the flaming gas-jet with his pocket handkerchief.

On another occasion during our Southern tour, Mr. McVicker called me on one side prior to the beginning of the last act of Hamlet, and whispered in my ear, "Watch me when I hand Edwin the skull to-night." I watched.

It appeared that our property-man had been unable to obtain even turnips with which to fashion skulls for the grave-yard scene, so he had procured a couple of very large Bermuda onions, cut and perforated them as he had done the turnips, colored, and placed them in the grave: Mr. McVicker alone being cognizant of the character of the remains. The grave-digger threw them out at the proper cue, and the deception passed unnoticed, but, when the old sexton handed the supposed skull of poor dead Yorick to Mr. Booth, who had a particular aversion to onions in any form, the aroma of that mutilated sphere, mingled with the odor of the paint, became so offensive to him that he was seized with nausea, and with difficulty completed the delivery of his tender apostrophe to the remains of his dead friend. However, his final questions to Horatio, as he handed, with unusual alacrity the repulsive vegetable to that gentleman: "Dost thou think Alexander looked o' this fashion i' the earth? And smelt so? pah!" had a significance that heretofore had not been in evidence. Subsequently Mr. Booth joined in a hearty laugh at the incident, and shortly afterwards two human skulls were purchased for the performance.

LAUNCE AND SPEED
IN
THE TWO GENTLEMEN OF VERONA

THERE seems to be little doubt but that the comedy of "The Two Gentlemen of Verona" was one of the earliest of the poet's dramatic works. There is no authentic record of its first presentation, but it is the general impression among the commentators that it occurred in 1591 or 1592. Sidney Lee, probably the most accurate and reliable authority on Shakespeareana, places it second in order of production. It was not printed in the author's lifetime, nor was it published till it was included in the First Folio edition of collected plays that appeared in 1623, seven years after the poet's death.

There is a crude conventionality in the construction of the plot, inexperience in the development of the characters, and immaturity in its deductive philosophy. These conditions confirm the view-point taken above, and are entirely consistent with the known facts. Shakespeare was at this time but twenty-seven years of age, had been in London but six or seven years, and though study and observation had given him some idea of dramatic composition, it was on conventional lines only; experience had not yet developed his powers or given him any marked individuality.

Mrs. Cowden Clarke goes so far as to suggest that the comedy was probably one of the MSS. that Shakespeare took with him to London. This is disproved, I think, by his references in the play to historical and mythological characters, with which he would hardly be familiar before his advent into the metropolis.

I doubt if Shakespeare did any literary work of a dramatic character before he went to London. It was his association with a company of professional actors, in a varied repertory of plays, with the environment of a regularly equipped theater, that revealed to him the possibilities of the drama, inspired his ambition, and developed his genius.

There is no originality in the story of "The Two Gentlemen of Verona," nor in any of the incidents of the comedy. The characters are but prototypes of those which appear, elaborated and completed, in his later plays, after experience had matured his powers and given him a deeper insight into human nature.

This is particularly true of Launce and Speed, the two clownish servants in the comedy, who are reproduced as the two Dromios, in "The Comedy of Errors"; as Peter, in "Romeo and Juliet," and as Launcelot Gobbo, in "The Merchant of Venice"; but with far more consistency of purpose and detail of character.

Launce and Speed are servants: born to serve, contented to serve, with little or no ambition beyond it. They are personal attendants on Valentine and Proteus, two young noblemen, and accompany their respective masters on their travels, obeying their orders without question, accepting their wages with satisfaction, and submitting upon occasion to personal chastisement without resentment.

They are young, full of humor, and fond of mischief. Their humor they exercise upon their masters, when they can do so with safety, and indulge in their mischief between themselves. Both are shrewd and keenly observant, particularly of the foibles and weaknesses of their masters.

Speed is at times exuberant; Launce, who is apparently the elder, is more thoughtful and sententious, and with the egotism of a little learning patronizes and reproves the youth and ignorance of his comrade. Launce has some sentimentality in his nature which is shown in his affection for his dog, Crab, and his grief (not wholly unaffected) at the parting from his family. Launce does not, however, permit that sentimentality to affect his material interests at any time, or even influence his considerations in the selection of a wife.

Both have the punning habit to an abnormal

degree, and vie with each other in amphibolous repartee.

Of the two, Launce has the keener wit and deeper philosophy. He is also more resourceful when occasion demands; witness, his prompt acceptance of the punishment that had been imposed on his "ungentlemanlike" dog, Crab, which would have ended the career of that canine; and the substitution of the same ill-bred cur for the "little jewel" he was commissioned to carry to Mistress Sylvia, which had been stolen from him by the boys in the market-place.

Speed is the first of these two worthies to appear in the play. It is in the first scene of the first act, and in his second speech he begins a corruption of words in a succession of the most atrocious puns and ingenious transliterations, that positively appall by their audacity: and he continues it throughout the scene. The play on the words, Ship and sheep, pound and pinfold, and the evolution from a nod of the head, and the exclamation "ay" to the word "Noddy," fully justifies the term Proteus applies to it, "silly."

In fact, there is but one bit of repartee in the entire dialogue worthy of note: Proteus exclaims with obvious sarcasm: "Beshrew me, but you have a quick wit," to which Speed, who has been unable to extract a gratuity from him, replies: "And yet it cannot overtake your slow purse."

The dialogue in Act 2, Scene 1, between Speed and Sir Valentine, is in the same vein as in the first act; but Speed seems to have some advantage in it, for travel appears to have sharpened the wit of the servant, while love has dulled the spirit of the master. In Speed there is evidence of more observation both of incidents and circumstances; a clearer and brighter expression of ideas, combined with a shrewdness that approaches wisdom, —especially in his reflections on Sir Valentine's love-lorn condition; while there is a dimness of comprehension that amounts almost to density in the lack of understanding displayed by his master. Speed's critical philosophy, however, never permits him to lose sight of the demands of his stomach, or the perquisites of his position.

This scene is so admirable in its commingling of humor and satire, that I quote it at length:

Val.   Why, how know you that I am in love?

Speed.   Marry, by these special marks.   First, you have learn'd, like Sir Proteus, to wreath your arms, like a malcontent; to relish a love-song, like a robin-redbreast; to walk alone, like one that had the pestilence; to sigh, like a schoolboy that had lost his A B C; to weep, like a young wench that had buried her grandam; to fast, like one that takes diet; to watch, like one that fears robbing; to speak puling, like a beggar at Hallowmas.   You were wont, when you laugh'd, to crow like a cock; when you walk'd, to walk like one of the lions; when you fasted, it was presently after dinner; when you look'd sadly, it was for want of money; and now you are metamorphosed with a mistress, that, when I look on you, I can hardly think you are my master.

Val.   Are all these things perceived in me?

Speed.   They are all perceived without ye. . . . These follies are within you, and shine through you like the water . . . that not an eye that sees you, but is a physician to comment on your malady.

Later, in the same scene the dialogue is note-worthy, and again illustrates the shrewd observance of Speed, and the privilege of speech permitted him by his master.

Speed. You never saw her since she was deform'd.

Val. How long hath she been deform'd?

Speed. Ever since you loved her.

Val. I have loved her ever since I saw her, and still I see her beautiful.

Speed. If you love her, you cannot see her.

Val. Why?

Speed. Because Love is blind. O! that you had nine eyes; or your own eyes had the lights they were wont to have, when you chid at Sir Proteus for gong ungartered!

Val. What should I see then?

Speed. Your own present folly, and her passing deformity; for he, being in love, could not see to garter his hose; and you, being in love, cannot see to put on your hose.

Sir Valentine, probably realizing the truth of Speed's remarks, and finding no adequate reply, attempts a reproof, which, however, does not teaze his irrepressible follower:

Val. Belike, boy, then you are in love; for last morning you could not see to wipe my shoes.

Speed. True, sir; I was in love with my bed. I thank you, you swinged me for my love, which makes me the bolder to chide you for yours.

Mistress Sylvia, the lady of Sir Valentine's love, now comes upon the scene, and Speed is a

most attentive observer and listener to the interview between the lover and the lady.   Sylvia has
apparently commissioned Sir Valentine to write
some appropriate lines for her to "one she loves,"
a "secret nameless friend."   Sir Valentine, having written the lines, in the form of a letter, now
delivers it to the lady, who thereupon returns it
to the writer, pointedly exclaiming: "They are
for you."   Sir Valentine, however, does not appreciate her meaning, looks bewildered and stands
in great perplexity; and the lady, disappointed at
his lack of comprehension, abruptly takes her
leave with considerable show of anger.   Sir Valentine stands in speechless astonishment, but Speed,
who has realized the full significance of the lady's
device, exclaims:

O jest unseen, inscrutable, invisible,
As a nose on a man's face, or a weathercock on a
    steeple!
My master sues to her, and she hath taught her suitor,
He being her pupil, to become her tutor.
O excellent device! was there ever heard a better,
That my master being scribe, to himself should write
    the letter.

James Lewis and Sidney Herbert as "Launce" and "Speed"
in "The Two Gentlemen of Verona"

Sir Valentine, still oblivious to the lady's design, and Speed's meaning, declares:

Val. Why, she hath not writ to me?

Speed. What need she when she hath made you write to yourself? Why, do you not perceive the jest?

Val. No, believe me.

Speed. Why, she hath given you a letter.

Val. That's the letter I writ to her friend.

Speed. And that letter hath she deliver'd, and there an end.

Val. I would it were no worse!

Speed. I'll warrant you, 'tis as well:

> For often have you writ to her, and she, in
>   modesty,
> Or else for want of idle time, could not
>   again reply;
> Or fearing else some messenger, that
>   might her mind discover,
> Herself hath taught her love himself to
>   write unto her lover.

Sir Valentine is still perplexed, he cannot see the jest, so Speed, seeing it impossible to make the matter clear, suggests: " 'Tis dinner time." Sir Valentine replies: "I have dined," but Speed requires a more substantial diet than love, and concludes the scene with the following most earnestly delivered protest: "Ay, but hearken, sir: Though the chameleon Love can feed on air, I am one that am nourish'd by my victuals, and would fain have meat. O! be not like your mistress: be moved, be moved."

Launce does not appear till the third scene of the second act, when he introduces himself, his sentiments, and his dog Crab, by whom he is accompanied, with much humor and, as with all of Shakespeare's characters, his mental, sentimental and social status is at once established; while the domestic drama played with a pair of old shoes, a hat, and a staff as representatives of the family of the Launces, gives us an introduction to them as effectively as if we had met them all in person. One can easily understand that Crab's failure to appreciate the importance of the journey, and the pathos of parting with such a family is a source of great disappointment to his master. The episode is described with so much delightful originality of expression and humorous detail, that the reader must be dull indeed who cannot see the scene enacted before his eyes: the weeping women, the wailing father, the howling maid, and the "perplexed" household; while the dog, unmoved, stolidly watches the entire proceedings with a bored expression of canine indifference.

Nay, 'twill be this hour ere I have done weeping: all the kind of the Launces have this very fault. I have received my proportion, like the prodigious son, and am going with Sir Proteus to the imperial's court. I think Crab my dog be the sourest-natured dog that lives: my mother weeping, my father wailing, my sister crying, our maid howling, our cat wringing her hands, and all our house in great perplexity, yet did not this cruel-hearted cur shed one tear: he is a stone, a very pebble-stone, and has no more pity in him than a dog: a Jew would have wept to have seen our parting: why, my grandam, having no eyes, look you, wept herself blind at my parting. Nay, I'll show you the manner of it: This shoe is my father;—no, this left shoe is my father; no, no, this left shoe is my mother: --that cannot be so neither: yes, it is so, it is so; it hath the worser sole. This shoe with a hole in it, is my mother, and this my father. A vengeance on't: there 't is: now, sir, this staff is my sister; for, look you, she is as white as a lily, and as small as a wand: this hat is Nan, our maid; I am the dog:—no, the dog is himself, and I am the dog,—O, the dog is me, and I am myself; ay, so, so. Now come I to my father; Father, your blessing; now should not the shoe speak a word for weeping; now should I kiss my father; well, he weeps on:—now come I to my mother, (O, that she could speak now, like a wood woman.)—well, I kiss her; why, there't is; here's my mother's breath up and down; now come I to my sister; mark the moan she makes: now the dog all this while sheds not a tear, nor speaks a word; but see how I lay the dust with my tears.

The misuse of the words "prodigious" and "perplexity" has a most familiar sound, and may be readily recognized as a favorite comedy device of the poet, to provide humor for his clowns and serving-men.

In an interesting work by Dr. A. O. Kellogg, of the State Lunatic Asylum, at Utica, New York, entitled "Shakespeare's Delineations of Insanity, Imbecility, and Suicide," that distinguished alienist places Launce among the imbeciles, and by way of preface to an able analysis of the character, in which is included Crab, the constant companion of the boy, he makes the following concrete summary:

Another shade of mental obtuseness and imbecility has been exhibited by the poet in the character of

Launce, the clown par excellence, in "The Two Gentlemen of Verona." Launce is not a character manu-
factured by the playwright, one of "Nature's journey-
men," to serve a particular purpose, but is a product
of Nature's own handiwork, and if not the most cunning, still none the less genuine.

The close companionship which exists between him
and his interesting dog, Crab, is evidently one based
upon a moral and intellectual fitness in the characters
of the two. The clown is such by natural organiza-
tion, and no education or change of circumstances or
condition could make him otherwise. So the dog
Crab, is . . . the cur that nature made him; and we
can scarcely conceive that even the cultivation of
three generations . . . would suffice to make either a
courtier of the one, or "a gentleman-like dog" of the
other. . . . The spirits of the two are so "married in
conjunction" by mutual intercourse, that the one has
come to conduct himself in all companies, as a currish
clown, and the other as a clownish cur.

As I have stated in the preface, I do not pre-
sume to differentiate between folly and imbecility. I quote the foregoing as the indorsement of
a scientist to the accuracy of the poet's conception
and treatment of the character.

In reference to the habit of punning, which is
one of the characteristics of Launce, to which I

have before alluded in this article, as well as to the same practice by similar characters in previous chapters, I again quote Dr. Kellogg:

His humorous punning and play upon words is also quite characteristic, and shows that this faculty may be possessed in quite an eminent degree by those of very inferior mental caliber, like Launce."

How completely Shakespeare realized this con‑ dition is evidenced, not only by the countrymen and clowns in his comedies, but also by the char‑ acters of inferior rank and humble station in his tragedies: notably, Peter, in "Romeo and Juliet"; the Citizens, in "Julius Cæsar"; the Grave-diggers, in "Hamlet"; and the drunker Porter, in "Mac‑ beth."

"The Two Gentlemen of Verona" is unfortu‑ nately seldom presented on the stage, but Mr. Augustin Daly made a production of the comedy in his series of Shakespearean revivals at Daly's Theater, New York, some years ago. Mr. James Lewis played Launce, and while I cannot recall the entire performance in detail, I distinctly remember his first appearance on the scene. He

came upon the stage slowly, with an expression
of extreme disgust on his face, leading his dog
Crab by a cord. The property man who had
procured the dog for the production had been
most fortunate in his selection, for a more complete specimen of a "low-down cur" I never saw.
It would have puzzled the most experienced dog
fancier to name his breed or trace his ancestry.
Most animals, when they appear upon the stage,
become frightened by the glare of the footlights,
and startled by any applause that may come from
the audience, but this dog that played Crab was
absolutely oblivious to his surroundings. Crab
received even a more cordial greeting than his
popular master, but while the latter acknowledged
the compliment gracefully, the dog looked on with
complete indifference as if the entire proceedings
bored him. Launce began his first speech, which
included a mild reproach of Crab's lack of sympathy, but it made no impression on the cur: he
then led the dog to the base of a statue, or foun-
tain on the scene, seated himself on the steps,
the cur by his side, and enacted the domestic scene

described in the text with a droll humor that the
audience found irresistible, but it had no effect
on Crab, who sat upon his haunches, looked at
Mr. Lewis' manipulation of the shoes, and listened to his detailed description of the parting of
the family of the Launces as if, like Baron Grog,
in "The Grand Duchess," he had always been
taught "to observe an impassive countenance."

I regret that I cannot remember more of the
performance of Mr. Lewis, for everything he did
was worthy of memory: but the picture of the
dog, Crab, is indelibly impressed on my mind, and
the memory of that frowsy cur that was such an
appropriate companion to his master, tempts me
again to quote Dr. Kellogg:

Next to the human associates whom a man takes
into his confidence, nothing seems to furnish a more
correct index to his character than the species of the
canine race which he selects as his companions. The
grim-looking, fighting bulldog is found at the heels
of the bully and prize-fighter. The dignified mastiff
and   gentlemanly   Newfoundland,   guard . . . the
stately banker. The gaunt hound is found in the train
of the active, vigorous, fox-hunting squire. The
poodle or spaniel . . . is the combed, washed, and

petted companion of my lady, but the cur, who seems to be a combination of the evil qualities of all these, your "yaller dog," is found at the heels of the clown, and the nature of the relationship is nowhere so admirably depicted as by the poet in his delineations of Launce and his dog Crab.

The play upon the words "tide" and "tied" in the brief dialogue with Panthino, that concludes the scene is another capital illustration of the quality of wit possessed by Launce. It is amusing, harmless and characteristic.

Pan. You'll lose the tide, if you tarry any longer.
Launce. It is no matter if the tied were lost; for it is the unkindest tied that ever any man tied.
Pan. What's the unkindest tide?
Launce. Why, he that's tied here, Crab, my dog.

Scene 5, of Act 2, is entirely occupied by a dialogue between Launce and Speed. The scene does not advance the plot or develop the characters, but is marked by the same quality of wit to which I have before referred; a brief example of which will suffice.

Speed. I understand thee not.
Launce. What a block art thou, that thou canst not. My staff understands me.

Speed. What thou sayest?

Launce. Ay, and what I do too: look thee, I'll but lean, and my staff understands me.

Speed. It stands under thee, indeed.

Launce. Why, stand-under and under-stand is all one.

In the first scene of act third a new phase of the character of Launce is developed. He is in love. We have his own admission of the fact, with the addenda: "But a team of horse shall not pluck that from me; not who 'tis I love, and yet 'tis a woman: but what woman, I will not tell myself; and yet 'tis a milkmaid." Launce does not give us his reasons for the secrecy that he so ingeniously negatives, and we might attribute it to the bashful modesty of a lover, but this is again negatived by his subsequent interview with Speed. The name of the lady is withheld, but we are frankly informed of "The cate-log of her conditions." Launce is a man of method and has carefully collated both the virtues and vices of the lady, and set them down in a sort of debtor and creditor arrangement, which he not only carefully considers himself, but on a convenient opportu·

r.ity submits to the judgment of his friend Speed, reserving, however, the privilege of making the final decision himself.

The merits of the lady are set down somewhat as follows:

She can fetch and carry.
She can milk.
She brews good ale.
She can sew.
She can knit.
She can wash and scour.
She can spin.
She hath many nameless virtues.

And her demerits:

She is not to be kissed fasting.
She hath a sweet mouth.
She doth talk in her sleep.
She is slow in words.
She is proud.
She hath no teeth.
She is curst.
She will often praise her liquor.
She is liberal.
She hath more hair than wit, and more faults than hairs, and more wealth than faults.

One can easily imagine the sapient and judicial air assumed by Launce, as Speed reads the "cate-log" to him; but I shrewdly suspect that the decision of the judge had been made before the trial began, or the evidence was presented. The virtues he appreciates at their practical value, the vices he ingeniously transforms into virtues, and like many in real life of far greater social and intellectual pretensions, finally permits the possession of money to be the deciding factor in his choice. With Launce, wealth appears to have been a cloak whose ample folds are sufficient to cover a multitude of vices, for though she have "more faults than hairs" her wealth was all powerful "to make the faults gracious." I am very much inclined, however, to think that the affectation of prudence was another of the practical jests of this exuberant youth with his friend Speed; that he himself concocted the "cate-log," and the entire matter had its existence only in the vivid and picturesque imagination of our friend Launce; for later we learn that the boy has voluntarily taken upon himself both the blame and the punishment for the sins of his dog Crab. He hath "sat in the stocks for puddings he hath stolen"; "stood in the pillory for geese he hath killed"; and taken a whipping to save that ill-bred cur from the consequences of his "ungentleman-like conduct" at the Duke's table. Now it is but reasonable to assume that a man, however humble his station in life, who would sacrifice himself so completely for the sake of a dumb animal, would have some sentimentality in the choice of a wife, and however mercenary he might assume to be, his selection would not be influenced by wealth alone, but be governed by the feelings of his heart, rather than by the calculations of his head.

Be that as it may, there is a good deal of sound common sense, even if it was assumed, in the method of selecting a wife as affected by Launce, that might be adopted with advantage by some of our modern young men who so heedlessly assume the responsibilities of marriage. A little more prudence and consideration of their respective qualifications for what should be a life-long union, might avert many an unhappy marriage, and considerably diminish the congestion in our courts of law.

The brief dialogue concluding the scene bears out the above suggestion. Speed, whose name by the way appears to be a misnomer, is waited for by his master at the north gate of the city. Launce knows this, and out of sheer mischief, as he inferentially admits, is detaining him. This would seem to indicate that the milkmaid with her "cate-log of conditions" is pure imagination on the part of Launce, and his apparent indecision a mere device to detain the already dilatory Speed. The solo and exit speech of Launce on the hasty departure of Speed, accentuates the view: "Now will he be swing'd for reading my letter. An unmannerly slave, that will thrust himself into secrets. I'll after, to rejoice in the boy's correction."

Scene 4 of Act 4 in the comedy brings the charactor of Launce to its conclusion. Crab seems to be as incorrigible as impenitent, and Launce entertains us with a most diverting account of the dog's misdeeds and his own self-sacrifice in the cur's behalf. To appreciate thoroughly the humor of the scene, I commend the reader to a full perusal of the same in the play itself.

By the irony of fate, Crab seems to be the factor in his master's undoing. Launce has been commissioned by his master, Sir Proteus, to deliver "a little jewel" of a dog to Mistress Sylvia as a present. Launce loses the little jewel, and in this dilemma substitutes his own dog Crab. The lady indignantly rejects such a present, and returns a most sarcastic response to the advances of the amorous Sir Proteus, whose anger on learning the details of the adventure may be better imagined than described.

The explanation of Launce is characteristic of the boy, while his humor, love of mischief, and his "old vice" of punning is sustained to the last.

Pro. Where have you been these two days loitering?

Launce. Marry, sir, I carried Mistress Sylvia the dog you bade me.

Pro. And what says she to my little jewel?

Launce. Marry, she says, your dog was a cur, and

tells you, currish thanks is good enough for such a present.

Pro. But she received my dog?

Launce. No, indeed, did she not: here have I brought him back again.

Pro. What, didst thou offer her this from me?

Launce. Ay, sir; the other squirrel was stolen from me by the hangman's boys in the market-place: and then I offered her mine own, who is a dog as big as ten of yours, and therefore the gift the greater.

Poor Launce narrowly escapes the whip at the hands of his outraged master, and is angrily dismissed from his presence. The future of the boy is left to our conjecture. Did he lose his place? Did his master restore him to favor? and did he wed the lady whose qualifications were the source of so much careful calculation? The author does not tell us. Let us, however, express the hope that an indulgent master forgave the exuberant humor of his youthful servant, and permitted Launce and his dog Crab, with possibly the lady Launce has chosen, to share in his own felicity so completely expressed in the concluding lines of the comedy, "One feast, one house, one mutual happiness."

THE FOOL
IN
KING LEAR

*"Poor fool and knave, I have one part in my heart
That's sorry yet for thee."*

*"The fool who labors to outjest
His heart-strook injuries."*

WHAT an exquisite picture the poet presents of the Fool in "Lear"! He has no name. He does not need one. It would lessen his significance. His age, his personality, are left to our imagination. Whether the tender pathos, the unswerving loyalty, the shrewd observance, the pointed parables, and the snatches of quaint old songs emanate from the soul of a youth or a man of maturity, we are not informed; but certain 'tis, the tears that force themselves through the fragments of melody and almost choke their utterance come from the loving heart of one whose affection time has tried and found sterling.

His master calls him "Boy," but that is from custom rather than fact; in the same sense that a negro servant in the South is called a "boy" till he dies of old age.

He has been a long time in the service of the king who evidently loves him, misses him from his train, and is impatient of his absence; for after repeatedly calling for him without reply, he abruptly demands: "But where's my fool? I have not seen him for these two days." That the Fool has penetrated the hypocritical protestations of the king's eldest daughters, Goneril and Regan, and learned to love the gentle but undemonstrative Cordelia is evidenced by the knight's reply: "Since my young lady's going into France, sir, the fool hath much pined away."

I picture the Fool as a young-old man, not as old as the king, of course; spare of body and of homely features, weak in frame but shrewd of mind; a gentle heart, full of gratitude for years of kindness and consideration at the hands of his semi-barbaric master; seeing with silent concern the gradual decay of a powerful personality; appalled by the mad king's disposition of his kingdom; impotent to save, but steadfast to soothe the subsequent sorrow and remorse of his deluded master.

Some of the recent commentators have found so much love and tenderness in the Fool for the king as to be almost filial, and have advanced the theory that Cordelia and the fool are one and the same person. This view I do not think is justified, either by the language or conditions. The only passage in the play that affords any authority for the theory is found in the last scene: Lear enters, carrying the body of Cordelia in his arms. He lays it upon the ground, and as he bends over the lifeless form of his daughter, he utters in his grief a number of broken phrases, among them the words: "And my poor fool is hanged." This may refer to Cordelia, for Shakespeare frequently uses the words, "poor fool," as a term of endearment, but I am of the opinion they have a literal meaning. The enemies of the king, knowing the loyalty and affectionate devotion of the Fool for his master, have hanged him; adding another sorrow to the over-burdened heart of the grief-stricken king.

In representing the play, I have always had the Fool present in the opening scene, a silent spectator of the disposition of the realm by the aged king, which seems to me consistent with the subsequent dialogue.

I directed him to run upon the scene following the entrance of the king and his court, but before the beginning of the dialogue, and with a merry salutation to his master to throw himself down at the foot of the throne. I instructed him to watch every motion, to listen intently to every word, and by facial expression silently but eloquently to reflect his emotions as the action of the scene proceeded. First, surprise at the king's division of the realm, awe at the terrible passion of his aged master, consternation at the dismissal of Kent, and horror at the denunciation and banishment of Cordelia. This business, together with his hardly suppressed gestures of protest and ap-

peal, and his final despair at his utter helpless-
ness to stem the torrent of the king's anger, I
found a most effective adjunct to the scene.   I
directed the Fool to linger on the scene after the
exit of the king and the court, and with dog-like
affection stealthily to creep over to the grief-
stricken, banished princess, furtively kiss the hem
of her robe, and then make his own exit from the
scene in sadness and silence.

The Fool disappears after Cordelia's departure
from the court with her husband, the King of
France, and hiding his grief is not seen again till
the growing impatience and repeated calls of his
master make his presence imperative.

In the fourth scene of the first act, Lear has
taken the disguised Earl of Kent into his service
as a reward for justly punishing an insolent follower of his daughter, when the Fool runs on, and
offering Kent his fools-cap, exclaims: "Let me
hire him, too: here's my coxcomb."

Kent, with good humored amusement, asks:
"Why, fool?"

To which the Fool answers: "Why, for taking one's part that's out of favor. Nay, and thou canst not smile as the wind sits, thou'lt catch cold shortly: there, take my coxcomb. Why, this fellow has banish'd two of his daughters, and did the third a blessing against his will; if thou follow him, thou must needs wear my coxcomb." I i.

The scene that follows is full of the deepest significance. The contrast between the gradually increasing anger of the king, that culminates in the terrible curse hurled on his daughter Goneril, and the pungent wit of the Fool, who, while he is unsparing with the lash of keenest satire, softens each blow with improvised lines of humor, and snatches of song (themselves the very quintessence of satire) is most striking. Epigrams, each more pointed than its predecessor, follow in rapid sequence, while the application of the couplets and doggerel to the situation is perfect; and yet, through it all there is a veiled tenderness, an indefinable sympathy that as we laugh at the wit, brings a tear of pity to the eye.

The scene is so full of wit, wisdom and sound philosophy, each phrase following the other with such cumulative precision, that I quote it almost in its entirety.

Fool. How now, nuncle? Would I had two coxcombs, and two daughters!

Lear. Why, my boy?

Fool. If I gave them all my living, I'd keep my coxcombs myself; there's mine; beg another of thy daughters.

Lear. Take heed, sirrah: the whip.

Fool. Truth's a dog must to kennel; he must be whipp'd out, when the lady brach may stand by the fire. . . . Sirrah, I'll teach thee a speech. Mark it nuncle:—

> Have more than thou showest,
> Speak less than thou knowest,
> Lend less than thou owest,
> Ride more than thou goest,
> Learn more than thou trowest,
> Set less than thou throwest;
> And thou shalt have more
> Than two tens to a score.

Kent. This is nothing, fool.

Fool. Then 'tis like the breath of an unfee'd lawyer; you gave me nothing for't. Can you make no use of nothing, nuncle?

Lear. Why, no, boy; nothing can be made out of nothing.

Fool. Pr'thee tell him, so much the rent of his land comes to; he will not believe a fool.

Lear. A bitter fool!

Fool. Dost thou know the difference, my boy, between a bitter fool and a sweet one?

Lear. No, lad; teach me.

Fool. That lord that counsell'd thee to give away
  thy land
  Come place him here by me, do thou for
   him stand;
  The sweet and bitter fool will presently appear;
  The one in motley here—the other found out
   there.   (*pointing to the King.*)

Lear. Dost thou call me fool, boy?

Fool. All thy other titles thou hast given away; that thou wast born with. . . . Nuncle, give me an egg, and I'll give thee two crowns.

Lear. What two crowns shall they be?

Fool. Why, after I have cut the egg i' the middle, and eat up the meat, the two crowns of the egg. When thou clovest thy crown i' the middle and gavest away both parts, thou borest thine ass on thy back o'er the dirt: thou had'st little wit in thy bald crown, when thou gavest thy golden one away.

 (*singing*) Fools had ne'er less grace in a year:
   For wise men are grown foppish;
   And know not how their wits to wear,
   Their manners are so apish.

Lear. When were you wont to be so full of songs, sirrah?

Fool. I have used it, nuncle, ever since thou mad'st

thy daughters thy mothers; for then thou gavest them the rod, and putt'st down thine own breeches,

 (*singing*) Then they for sudden joy did weep,
     And I for sorrow sung,
     That such a king should play bo-peep
     And go the fools among.

Prythee, nuncle, keep a schoolmaster that can teach thy fool to lie; I would fain learn to lie.

Lear. An you lie, sirrah, we'll have you whipp'd.

Fool. I marvel what kin thou and thy daughters are; they'll have me whipp'd for speaking true, thou'lt have me whipp'd for lying; and sometimes I am whipp'd for holding my peace. I had rather be any kind o' thing than a fool: and yet I would not be thee, nuncle; thou hast pared thy wit o' both sides, and left nothing in the middle. Here comes one o' the parings.

At this point Goneril, the king's eldest daughter, comes upon the scene; she is apparently very angry, and her feelings are reflected in her countenance, for the king challenges her:

Lear. How now, daughter? what makes that frontlet on? Methinks you are too much of late i' the frown.

Before Goneril can reply, and much to the manifest indignation of that lady, subsequently expressed, the "all-licensed" Fool accurately sums up the situation.

Fool. Thou wast a pretty fellow when thou hadst no need to care for her frowning; now thou art an O without a figure: I am better than thou art now: I am a fool, thou art nothing.—
    Mum, mum,
    He that keeps nor crust nor crumb,
    Weary of all, shall want some.

Goneril's wrath now breaks forth in a most bitter and vituperative speech to her father, the insolence and audacity of which strikes the old king momentarily dumb. The Fool, however, is neither surprised nor affrighted, but exclaims:

Fool. For you know, nuncle,
    The hedge-sparrow fed the cuckoo so long,
    That it's had its head bit off by its young.

With consummate art, the poet has gradually eliminated the humor and satire as the tragic passion of the situation increases; but he has reserved one line to the Fool that to me is awful in its significance, and connotes limitless possibilities of thought and conjecture. Lear, appalled at the audacity and disrespect of his daughter, doubts

the evidence of his eyes and his ears, his personality, his very existence; and exclaims: "Does
any here know me? Who is it that can tell me
who I am?"

To which the Fool replies: "Lear's shadow."

The words seem to carry corroboration with
them; for instead of the powerful monarch whose
will was law, and word a command, we see before
us a weak, indefinite remainder of something
which was a personality, and now is nothing;
nothing but a shadow; realizing but too late the
fatal error that robbed him of the power he is now
impotent to regain. Something, however, of his
old self returns as insults accumulate on his reverend head; the limit of even paternal endurance
is reached, and the outraged father hurls on the
head of his thankless child a curse, the terrific
force of which is probably unequaled in literature,
and leaves her.

Goneril orders the Fool to follow him: "You,
sir, more knave than fool, after your master."

The Fool obeys, leaving, however, his compliments behind him.

> A fox, when one has caught her,
> And such a daughter,
> Should sure to the slaughter,
> If my cap would buy a halter;
> So the fool follows after.

Loyally the faithful Fool follows his master; with tender solicitude he strives, by quip and quaint reply, to divert the remnant of the poor king's mind from the deep grief that envelops it, and by folly "labors to outjest his heart-strook injuries." The effort, however, is but partially successful; the deep sorrow beneath absorbs the rippling laughter on the surface and dissolves it into tears.

How pathetic are the steadfast efforts of the Fool to change the current of the old king's thoughts, and dull the constantly recurring memories of his wrongs. As one witty suggestion fails to hold his attention, the Fool flits to another; a jest, a riddle, a pun, anything that will stifle the sob, hold back the tear, or deaden the memory. Not folly for folly's sake, but to allay the pain of a breaking heart. This is comedy brought into such close relation with the grea

sorrows of life that it is transformed to the deepest tragedy.   Combination and contrast!   A king
and a fool!   Reverence and folly!   Majesty and
motley!   Weakness   protecting   strength!   A
clown defending a scepter, and a bauble shielding
a crown; and yet all of these contrasts are har-
monized by the holiest of human emotions, fidelity and love.

How significant are the lines, how clear their
purpose!

Fool.   Shalt see thy other daughter will use thee
kindly; for though she's as like this as a crab's like an
apple, yet I can tell what I can tell.
Lear.   What canst tell, boy?
Fool.   She will taste as like this as a crab does to
a crab.   Thou canst tell why one's nose stands i' the
middle on's face?
Lear.   No.
Fool.   Why, to keep one's eyes of either side's
nose; that what a man cannot smell out he may spy
into.

Here, the king's mind reverts to the banishment of his daughter Cordelia:

Lear.   I did her wrong:—

But the Fool changes the current of his thoughts by another question:

Fool. Canst tell how an oyster makes his shell?
Lear. No.
Fool. Nor I neither: but I can tell why a snail has a house.
Lear. Why?
Fool. Why, to put his head in; not to give it away to his daughters, and leave his horns without a case.

Again the memory of his grief returns, and again the Fool provides a diversion:

Lear. I will forget my nature.—So kind a father!—Be my horses ready?
Fool. Thy asses are gone about 'em. The reason why the seven stars are no more than seven is a pretty reason.
Lear. Because they are not eight?
Fool. Yes, indeed; thou wouldst make a good fool.

However Lear might have appreciated this doubtful compliment, in his normal mental condition, it is lost on him now, and his thoughts are once more on his wrongs:

Lear. To tak't again perforce!—Monster ingratitude!

Once more the Fool recalls him from himself:

Fool. If thou wert my fool, nuncle, I'd have thee beaten for being old before thy time.

Lear. How's that?

Fool. Thou shouldst not have been old till thou hadst been wise.

The horses are now brought out, and the king, with the Fool, and his reduced train of fifty followers start on their journey.

With untiring devotion the Fool follows the wandering way of the king, hovering near his side and lightening the journey with jest and song, diverting his old master's mind from its heavy sorrow by numberless devices, till they reach the castle of Gloster, where Regan, the king's second daughter, and her husband, the Duke of Cornwall, are visitors.

Though the king's visit is not unexpected, the gates are closed, no preparation is made for his reception, and his arrival is unheralded. His messenger, the disguised Kent, whom he had sent before to announce his coming, is set in the stocks before the entrance to the castle; a degradation and punishment reserved—only for the basest of men. The Fool is the first to observe this, and realizing at once the outrage on the dignity of the king by the stocking of his messenger, endeavors to dwarf the affront by turning it to folly:

Fool. Ha, ha; he wears cruel garters! Horses are tied by the head; dogs and bears by the neck; monkeys by the loins; and men by the legs; when a man is over lusty at legs, then he wears wooden nether-stocks.

But the insult is too apparent, the outrage too flagrant, to be overlooked; the king demands an explanation from his servant, which being given, indicates further indignities, and provokes from the Fool the following sage reflections:

Fool. Winter's not gone yet, if the wild geese fly that way.
    Fathers that wear rags do make their children blind;
    But fathers that bear bags shall see their children kind.

Lear, commanding his train to remain without enters the castle to seek his daughter. Kent, still in the stocks, noting the reduced number of the king's attendants, asks:

Kent. How chance the king comes with so small a number?

To which the Fool replies:

Fool. An thou hadst been set i' the stocks for that question, thou hadst well deserved it.
Kent. Why, fool?

The answer to Kent's question contains so much of bitter truth, worldly wisdom and sound reasoning, that the speaker might well be a grave and reverend man of age, deducing his philosophy from a life-long experience, rather than a motley fool venting his folly for the diversion of the moment.

Fool. We'll set thee to school to an ant, to teach thee there's no laboring i' the winter. All that follow their noses are led by their eyes, but blind men. Let go thine hold when a great wheel runs down a hill, lest it break thy neck with following; but the great one that goes up the hill, let him draw thee after. When a wise man gives thee better counsel, give me mine again: I would have none but knaves follow it, since a fool gives it.

> That sir which serves and seeks for gain,
> And follows but for form,
> Will pack when it begins to rain,

And leave thee in the storm.
But I will tarry; the fool will stay,
And let the wise man fly:
The knave turns fool that runs away;
The fool no knave, perdy.

Take the above, phrase by phrase, note its application and significance; the bitter reflections of the Fool on the disloyalty of the king's former friends; the doubts of his present followers; the truisms of wisdom and folly; the more than suggestion of knavery; and the declaration of his own devotion, that in another might appear egotistically effusive, but in the fool is natural and sincere.

But I will tarry; the fool will stay,
And let the wise man fly.

The reply to Kent's query is certainly true. The lesson was well learned, but "Not i' the stocks, fool."

The Fool is silent during the scene that follows, and allows the indignation of the king to have full sway without interruption, till passion gives way to grief; this he tries to stay with the jest of the cockney and the eels and the butter'd hay, but the great flood of an outraged father's wrath is beyond his power to stem. Awestricken and dumb he stands, impotently watching the sturdy defense of his aged master against the combined attack of his unnatural daughters. Powerless to shield him from a single blow, he sees his strength waning, and his reason totter, till the limit of human endurance is reached, and the old man, exhausted in mind and body, falls into the arms of his humble friend with the agonizing cry, "O, fool, I shall go mad!"

The gates, like the hearts of his "pernicious daughters," are closed against him; night falls, and the storm descends. "The fretful elements contend," "the to-and-fro conflicting wind and rain," struggle for supremacy, and vent their fury on the earth.

The Fool is not consistent; he has not taken his own advice to "Let go thine hold when a great wheel runs down a hill," but clings to the descending and revolving disk as it rolls to destruction.

The rain drenches him to the skin, the wind

chills his blood to ice, and the flashing fire and rolling thunder fill his heart with fear; but the combined fury of the elements cannot drive him from his master's side, or shake the loyalty of his love. Patiently he follows the aimless footsteps of the distracted king, clinging to his dripping garments, and, first by suggestion and then appeal, endeavors to guide the grief-stricken old man to shelter.

Fool. O nuncle, court holy-water in a dry house is better than this rain-water out o' door. Good nuncle in; ask thy daughters' blessing; here's a night pities neither wise men nor fools.

Yet both are abroad, exposed to its impetuou blasts.

How well our poet knew that contrast was and is, the very essence of the drama; and hov strikingly the contrasts of life are here presented Great nature in the majesty of its wrath, wea humanity at its mercy! The deep philosophy o a child-changed father, and the trifling jests of motley clown! A witty fool, and a witless king and yet these contrasts are woven into the fabri of the play with such consummate skill that a natural and perfect harmony is preserved.

Truly there is wisdom beneath the coxcomb in the following:

He that has a house to put's head in has a good head-
  piece.

That man that makes his toe
What he his heart should make
Shall of a corn cry woe,
And turn his sleep to wake.

For there was never yet fair woman but she made
  mouths in a glass.

Truisms but trifles! yet they form the only remedy the poor Fool can offer to cure the deadly grief of the old king; the only stay his puny strength can put forth to prevent that "great wheel" from running down the hill.

We recognize the truth of the boy's reply to the demand of Kent upon the heath, "Who's there?" "Marry, here's grace and a cod-piece; that's a wise man and a fool." But we reverse the intent of the assertion.

Kent succeeds in inducing the old king to seek

some shelter, and the fool and the knave lead him unresistingly to the hovel.

> The art of our necessities is strange,
> That can make vile things precious.

Foul straw that has bedded cattle is the pallet of a king, and his chamber a hovel that a swine-herd would despise; yet the royalty of his nature reigns within his heart, and regal grace still shines about him. In his great extremity the fidelity of his friends is not forgotten; nothing could be more tender than his gracious acknowledgment of his love and appreciation, ere he seeks the humble shelter they have found for him:

> Poor fool and knave, I have one part in my heart
> That's sorry yet for thee.

Oh! faithful Fool! unselfish friend! thou need'st not the sunlight of fortune to develop thy love; storms may fright thee; cold may chill thy blood; and fear invade thy heart, but thou art steadfast.

The elements themselves approve thy fidelity, and abate their fury, for the storm grows less severe; and above the soughing of the wind the sweet melody of thy gentle song, infected with thy tears fills the air with the soft tranquillity of a mother's lullaby, and soothes the vexed spirit of thy much loved master.

> He that has and a little tiny wit,
> With hey, ho, the wind and the rain,
> Must make content with his fortunes fit,
> Though the rain it raineth every day.

How true to nature is the reaction.   The king is sheltered, at least for a time; for himself or his own ease the Fool has no thought, so the keen edge of his wit is directed to the world and its injustices.   How bitterly cynical his arraignment of fortune, an indictment that in its quality is so comprehensive and prophetic, it would seem as if the poet's vision had pierced the veil of time, and named the wrongs and corruptions of the present day.

The Fool is alone and his thoughts are expressed in the nature of a soliloquy:

> I'll speak a prophecy ere I go:
> When priests are more in word than matter;

When brewers mar their malt with water;
When nobles are their tailors' tutors;
No heretics burn'd, but wenches' suitors; .
When every case in law is right;
No squire in debt, nor no poor knight;
When slanders do not live in tongues;
Nor cutpurses come not to throngs;
When usurers tell their gold i' the field;
And bawds and wantons churches build:
Then shall the realm of Albion
Come to great confusion:
Then comes the time, who lives to see't,
That going shall be us'd with feet.

It will be observed that the above is the first soliloquy of the Fool, in other words, the first time that, being alone, he has spoken his thoughts that we might know them.

As a rule, I have found in Shakespeare the first soliloquy to be the keynote to the character; but I think the present instance is an exception. The shrewd satire of the parabolical epigrams that the Fool has uttered with so much deliberation would indicate a worldly wisdom and embittered sarcasm, rather than the loyalty and love which is his distinguishing characteristic, and which seems to expand and grow as the poor old king's strength fails, and wits give way.

Once more the king is out in the storm, and now another character is added to the scene—"Poor Tom," the Bedlam beggar, whose exaggerated ravings make an appropriate addition to the environment, and complete the picture of human misery.

Small wonder that, appalled by the combination by which he is surrounded, the Fool exclaims: "This cold night will turn us all to fools and madmen."

What a trio of contrast is presented at the rude farmhouse in which they are now sheltered: The poor old king, his clothing torn by the briers, his hair and beard ravished by the wind, rain-soaked to the skin, and growing more witless every minute; the naked Bedlam beggar (Edgar disguised), "Poor Tom," assuming madness for safety; and the motley fool, serving and suffering with dog-like fidelity, content to share his master's fortune, be it good or ill. Among them it is indeed difficult to determine who is sane, and who is not, and the declaration of the Fool seems to be apt and appropriate: "He's mad that trusts in the tameness of a wolf, a horse's health, a boy's love, or a wanton's oath."

The composition of the court of justice, in the old farmhouse, of a serving man, a beggar, and a Fool on the bench, commissioned by a mad king to try imaginary offenders, forms a most "honorable assembly," and is indeed a grim satire on the administration of justice.

It may be observed, that while Shakespeare has treated the Chief Justice in Henry IV, and the higher judges, if so I may term them in his several plays, with respect and dignity, he is very severe on the ignorance and arrogance of the petty justices and local magistrates. How far this may be due to his own experience with several Warwickshire justices, with whom it is said he became somewhat unpleasantly familiar in his youth, and against whom he appears to have retained some resentment all his life, I am not prepared to say.

The long, long day of sorrow, pain and suffering comes to an end at last. "Oppressed nature"
has reached the limit of its endurance, her "foster-
nurse," repose, has "closed the eye of anguish,"
and compassionate sleep, the "balm of hurt
minds," brings oblivion, for a time at least.

The king falls asleep, his clouded mind mur-
muring, "We'll go to supper i' the morning," and
the faithful Fool, his limbs benumbed with cold,
his eyes wearied with watching and his heart
heavy with grief, responds, "And I'll go to bed
at noon."

These are the last lines spoken by the Fool; the
litter to carry the king to a place of safety is prepared; the Fool, at Kent's command, assists the
others to bear away his sleeping master, and is
seen no more. No further reference is made to
him, and we are left in ignorance of his fate if
we except a brief passage spoken by the king in
the last scene of the tragedy: "And my poor fool
is hanged."

Commentators as I have said, differ as to the
application of these words. Some claim that

they refer to his dead daughter Cordelia, but I prefer to regard them as informing us of the fate of the poor Fool, whose life has been sacrificed to his fidelity.

It is but a natural conclusion, and in perfect harmony with the tragic incidents of the play. Such love, such unselfish devotion could not survive its object. It was inevitable. Life with such tragic memories would be impossible to endure. No. One fate encompassed them both. The gentle spirit of the faithful friend has gone before, and patiently waits for the poor tortured soul of his loved master to share the peace that he has found.

> He that hath a little tiny wit,—
> With heigh, ho, the wind and the rain;
> Though the rain it raineth every day,
> Oh the wind, the wind and the rain.

THE END

ImTheStory.com

Personalized Classic Books in many genre's

Unique gift for kids, partners, friends, colleagues

Customize:

- • Character Names

- • Upload your own front/back cover images (optional)

- • Inscribe a personal message/dedication on the
  inside page (optional)

Customize many titles Including
- • Alice in Wonderland
- • Romeo and Juliet
- • The Wizard of Oz
- • A Christmas Carol
- • Dracula
- • Dr. Jekyll & Mr. Hyde
- • And more...

Lightning Source UK Ltd.
Milton Keynes UK
UKOW031826200313

207957UK00019B/821/P